LETTERS OF AL-GHAZZALI

LETTERS OF AL-GHAZZALI

ABDUL QAYYUM

KITAB BHAVAN
New Delhi-110002

KITAB BHAVAN
Exporters & Importers
1784, Kalan Mahal, Daryaganj
New Delhi-110002 [India]

Phones : *3274686, 3263383*
Telex : *31-63106 ALI IN*
Fax : *91-11-3274686*

ISBN 81-7151-155-4

First Published in India 1992
2nd Edition : 2008

Published by:
Nusrat Ali Nasri for Kitab Bhavan
1784, Kalan Mahal, Daryaganj
New Delhi-110002 [India]

Printed in India at:
Nazia Printers
Rodgran, Lal Kuan
Delhi-110006

CONTENTS

PREFACE

Imam Al-Ghazzali has related in one of his immortal works entitled *Manqidh minad Dalal* (Deliverer from Error) all that he endured in seeking to recover the truth from amidst the confusion of sects with diverse ways and paths, till he finally raised himself from the abyss of blind belief in the authority to the height of discernment, where his entranced soul pierced the veil of illusion and stood in the presence of Truth itself and the light fell distinctly on his heart. This book is an arresting collection of the Imam's letters addressed to the Saljuqi sovereigns, viziers, princes and the learned men of his time including the famous chief minister Hasan b. 'Ali, the great Nizamul Mulk Tusi (the friend of 'Umar Khayyam and vizier successively to Sultan Alp Arslan and to his son Jalaluddin Malik Shah) who was the most capable administrator, acute statesman, a liberal patron of letters and sincere friend to men of letters. These epistles are being rendered into English for the first time. In them is reflected a complete self-realization of one of the most remarkable reformers of his days who refused to bow before an immoral power. As a young man he rebelled against formal religion yet he was deeply religious. He gave his wise advise to kings, governors and other government officials and brought down heavens of wrath and invective upon exploiters, un-sympathetic rulers and corrupt officials, political, ecclesiastical and others employing improper use of power and position. He discovered that unless he first reformed himself and got rid of certain spiritual ills from which he himself was suffering, he could effectively reform the rulers and common man and teach the basic principles of a universal import, directing the evolution of human society on a spiritual basis. That is why the hatred of this world and love of the Lord forced him to renounce the pomp and glory of the world, to become a wandering dervish in search of truth, at a time when his worldly prospects were brilliant as a Grand Mufti of the Saljuq empire and a famous professor of the Nizamiya College. Had he not dedicated his life entirely to the service of the mankind, he could not have been bold enough to rebuke Muinul Mulk, one of the Saljuqi viziers for drinking wine and mis-using the public money and leading a luxurious life.

Of course, the letters are a source of great interest as these deal with great contemporary events in history. That is why our interest in these letters increases, when we find Al-Ghazzali reprimanding the Saljuqi sovereigns and their ministers against all compromises with corruption, nepotism, favouritism, injustice and bribery which were the main ills of the society in those days.

In one of these letters he speaks of the sad state of affairs of the then existing human society (1120 A.D.) which seem to be appropriate for the modern age.

The cry of all the miserable and the lamentation of the helpers can no longer be heard by those administrating the affairs of the State. Will peace be on earth, while the poor people are working to feed the strong and fill the stomachs of the tyrants? Will studies for historical and mystical information. It has won its place among the Persian readers as a beautiful autograph portrait of Al-Ghazzali who by natural charm of his mysticism is as much alive for us today, as he was to his disciples during his lifetime. His thoughts are universal and he will certainly live on and grow through the centuries, as the impact of his genius increases with the passage of time. There is no doubt that today's striferidden world, full of deceit, prejudices and hypocrisy badly needs Al-Ghazzali's message of peace, love, selflessness and universal brotherhood. In the matter of style there is no comparison between him and his contemporaries, who being self-conceited endeavoured to write in a style of turgid verbosity with the deliberate intention of concealing their real feelings and motives. They could not be generally understood, because instead of trying to make difficult things easy of comprehension, they made things, which were easy in themselves difficult, to be comprehended by the manner in which they presented them. The real charm of Al-Ghazzali's letters is that they are obviously frank and sincere, with nothing to conceal and without verbosity. Like all else he wrote on the subject of mysticism. They are easy and vivid, showing a glowing zeal for the improvement of the condition of the poor and for the welfare of his fellow-men.

It is much to be regretted that in spite of selfless efforts, it has not been found possible either to ascertain the exact dates, when these letters were written or traced out the places from which they were addressed, though presumably several of them seem to have been written from his native town Tus in Khurasan, to which place he had retired. It remains briefly to describe the source from which the present book has been translated. The mass of Al-Ghazzali's published correspondence is enormous and lies scattered in Arabic and Persian books like *Tabaqat-i-Shafi'a*. *Majma'ul Insha* and *Aasarul Wuzara'*, etc. But the most important collection of his letters is obtainable in a Persian book entitled *Faza'ilul Anam Min Rasa'il-i-Hujjatul Islam* which ascribe of Al-Ghazzali's own city and claiming close relationship with him, selected and copied out in his old age. I have throughout translated the full text of every letter as given in the authority from which it has been taken.

As, however, everyone of these twenty-six letters is included in the oldest MS. now in the Constantinople University Library, the reader is assured that the text of the original Persian letters is equally the oldest and, therefore, the most authentic version available.

Abbottabad

ABDUL QAYYUM

INTRODUCTION

In the name of God, the Most Merciful, the Most Compassionate and blessings be upon Muhammad, the Prophet of Allah and as well as on his family and his companions, who led us forth from error!

Al-Ghazzali is a figure of such towering importance that some detailed account of his life, doctrine and works must be inserted in a book like this which professes to be a collection of his selected letters.

Imam Abu Hamid Muhammad, Al-Ghazzali, the *Shafi'ite* and *Ash'arite*, was born at Tus in Khurasan in 450 A.H. (1072 A.D.) about the time of Sultan Alp Arslan's accession to the Seljuq's throne, and died at the age of fifty-five in the year 1127 A.D. at Tabaran, a village near Tus. The latter was in ancient times one of the famous cities in Khurasan. It is today little more than a village, but is well known for its association with the famous poet Firdausi who died there in 1020 A.D. Al-Ghazzali's father himself was an illiterate person, but appears to have been remarkably careful of his son's education. He used to spin wool and sell it in his shop. That is why the family of Al-Ghazzali, is known as such, since its members were the spinners of wool.

The father of Al-Ghazzali entrusted his two sons Al-Ghazzali himself and his brother Ahmad to the care of a pious sufi who taught them writing and educated them till the money left by him was spent up. They were taught and brought up in quite poor and humble conditions and it became impossible for them to continue their studies.

Then says Al-Ghazzali, "Our teacher with whom we had lived before, turned us out of his doors and we did not like to be a source of burden to him, so we left his house. Disappointed and disheartened we had to leave our hearth and home and went to a college to learn jurisprudence so that we might gain our livelihood".

After staying in the college for some time Al-Ghazzali made for Jurjan where he learnt the fundamentals of the current subjects at the feet of Nasr Al-Isma'ili. While coming back from Jurjan something happened that made life-long impact on Al-Ghazzali. In these days, the life of a scholar was beset with hardships and difficulties. Many students had set out, as a matter of course, on a journey of a thousand mile or more in quest of a teacher. Vast journeys from Spain to Mecca and from Baghdad to Morocco were undertaken by young man who left their homes practically penniless to sit at the feet of a chosen master.

R.R. Nicholson says in his learned work '*A Literary History of the Arabs*' that "it seemed as if all the world from the Caliph down to the humblest citizen suddenly became students or at least patrons of literature. In quest of knowledge men travelled over three continents and returned home, like bees laden with honey, to impart the precious stores which they accumulated to crowds of eager disciples and to compile with incredible industry. Those works of encyclopaedic range and erudition from which modern science, in the widest sense of the word had derived far more than is generally supposed" (pp. 21, 22). As he was coming back from Jurjan, his caravan was waylaid by robbers and in the loot he lost his very precious note-book. The young scholar got so much agitated at the loss of his only "treasure" that he follows them to crave the return of his lecture-notes, "for which" said he "I left my home and which contain my knowledge". Thereat, the chief robber laughed and said, "How does thou pretend to have acquired the knowledge contained in them which we have snatched from thee, thou art robbed of thy knowledge and left knowledgeless?"

And thereafter, Al-Ghazzali, having recovered his note-book did not rest, till all their contents had been learnt and fully assimilated. His memory had become so prodigious now that he could repeat from his memory whatever he learnt in the books without making any mistake. Sometimes he could reproduce ten or eleven pages of a prose work over which he had cast one hasty glance, so that as he said, "should I again be robbed, I should not be deprived of my knowledge."

Thereafter he went to Nishapur to become a disciple of 'Abdul Malik Juraini widely known as 'Abdul Malik Ma'ali Imamul Haramain, who was appointed as a Vice Chancellor of the well-known Nizamiya University in Baghdad. He was the man who had a big say in the Government of the day. After teaching Al-Ghazzali for some time he left the country in consequences of Alp Arslan's vizier Imadul Mulk at Kunduri's having obtained the permission of his master to have curses pronounced against the *Ash'arites* (to which sect both Al-Ghazzali and Imamul Haramain belonged) from the pulpits of Khurasan. To escape the curses Imamul Haramain went to Mecca and Medina, where he was held in the highest esteem as a great *Imam* who appeared on ceremonial occasions, attended by a numerous train of admiring disciples. He wielded a tremendous spiritual influence over the people.

The great Nizamul Mulk exhorted himself on behalf of the *Ash'arites* and the Nizamiya College; Baghdad which was designed to propagate the *Ash'arite* school of theology till he stamped it with the impression of his own powerful genius, shaped its pattern and established it as the universal creed of orthodox Islam. Having learnt that things had settled down to a normal form and peace restored, Imamul Haramain came back to Baghdad, and Al-Ghazzali resumed his studies under him. He learnt all available knowledge from his teacher, made tremendous strides and completely hypnotised the Persian mind with his intellectual superiority, till he outshone his own teacher. It is reliably reported that when Al-Ghazzali wrote his book *Mankhul* and presented it to his teacher for his opinion about the work, Imamul Haramain exclaimed with grief, when he read it thoroughly "Alas! you have eclipsed my fame as a writer to such an extent that I feel as if I were dead". At his death Imamul Haramain left several prominent works and four hundred distinguished scholars as pupils, but Al-Ghazzali surpassed them all. During the lifetime of his teacher he had become a mobile treasure-house of learning, a legend, a living institution carving out a sure niche for himself in the edifice of mysticism. He visited such places as Damascus, Jerusalem, Cairo and Alexandria, which were highly flourishing cities in those days and were famous centres of learning and culture. He also lectured and taught at these places and his books and treatises on various subjects were widely read and appreciated.

On the death of his teacher he set out for the camp-court of the Seljuq monarch Malik Shah, son of the Sultan Alp Arslan, and presented himself to the Nizamul Mulk whose assembly was the alighting place of the learned and destination of the leading divines and servants, and there he enjoyed the society of the principal doctors and rebutted his opponents in matters of religious controversy despite their eminence. Thereafter, there were long sessions during which he debated brilliantly on such philosophical and religious subjects as life, death, creation, prayers and evolution etc.

So the Nizamul Mulk was inclined to him and showed him great respect and honour by appointing him a Professor in the Nizamiya College which he had founded at Baghdad twenty-five years before the Norman Conquest of England.

Al-Ghazzali became so powerful that no affair of the State could be deemed settled without his approval. In recognition of his great services to the cause of Islam, the Seljuq monarch Malik Shah is reported to have loged him in apartments in the royal palace and fixed him handsome salary for being a Mufti of the Seljuq empire. He honoured him with an official robe, till his influence soon exceeded that of the Amirs and viziers. Al-Ghazzali's friend Allama 'Abdul A'afir al-Farsi, Khatib of Nishapur described Al-Ghazzali "as the chief man in Baghdad, very rich, revered by the inhabitants and surrounded by more than three hundred students who came from all parts of the Muslim world to attend his lectures on *Sufiism* and theology. His fame has burst like the uncontrollable light of the tropical sun on a mid-summer dawn. The world is dazzled by it." The same authority continued to describe him "as being possessed of extraordinary self-control, strict in the performance of his religious duties, secretive, harsh and stern and even proud of an exceedingly aggressive and domineering manner when occasion arose, but at other times very generous even towards his foes."

Thus Al-Ghazzali was riding the high tide of the world fame and prominence, when something very spectacular happened to give a new turn to his whole life.

One day as he was reading *Nahjul Balagha* a collection of Hazrat 'Ali's sermons, he came across these lines.

"Let me warn you that the things like wealth, power, pleasures which crafty impostors and knavish seducers have surrounded themselves with may not allure and tempt you because life is like a shadow across the earth which before finally disappearing may lengthen for some time, but will ultimately fade away. Cast aside your vanity and remember that he who humbles himself will be exalted and he who exalts himself will be crushed".

His lofty soul recoiled from worldly vanities and the spirit of earnest loving for a solid rock on which to rest the weary soul, spoke to his heart, therefore, at the height of his splendour, he renounced all pomp and power and suddenly disappeared from the midst of his companions in order to give himself up to devotion and dervishhood and to seek a kingdom of eternal tranquillity. This rigid attitude cost him heavily and shattered his nerves. Nevertheless it brought him closer to the realities of life. He set out in the year 1905 A.D. for Hijaz. On his return form the pilgrimage he journeyed to Damascus and stayed there for ten years in the minaret of the congregational Mosque and composed several works of which *Ihya'ul-'Ulum* is said to be one. There he also devoted himself to worship and constant recitation of the Holy Qur'an and dissemination of knowledge and shunned company of people. Then after visiting Jerusalem and Alexandria, he returned to his home at Tus where he founded a university for training and preparing scholars and revolutionaries who could provide the necessary guidance and leadership to the world of Islam. The vizier Fakhrul Mulk, the son of Nizamul Mulk came to see him and urged him by every means in his power to accept professorship in the Nizamiya College at Nishapur. It may not be out of place to mention here that there were two Nizamiya Colleges founded by Nizamul Mulk--one at Baghdad and the other at Nishapur. Al-Ghazzali consented and his return to public life took place in 1106 A.D. but after teaching for some time resigned from the post and returned to end his days in his native town. It was during this period of his stay at Nishapur that a controversial question arose between him and

'Omar Khayyam, the famous author of the Persian quatrains who was one of Al-Ghazzali's contemporaries and co-thinker in Persian. It is reported that one day as Ghazzali met 'Omar Khayyam, he was asked by the latter to give his opinion on a point regarding the mysteries of the human soul. Al-Ghazzali explained that the human soul perceives things and perception is a quality which must exist in substance. It cannot exist by itself. As soul is not a body, it cannot be described and, therefore, it is named in the Holy Qur'an as "the Command of God."

'Omar Khayyam, who was extremely critical of the sufis refuted him saying that when the sufis cannot score a point, they resort to the quotations from the Qur'an which cannot satisfy a free thinker. Meanwhile the call of the Muezzin (to prayer) came. Referring to the call of the Muezzin Al-Ghazzali recited the following verses from the Holy Qur'an, "Truth hath come and falsehood hath vanished away, Lo! falsehood is ever bound to vanish." (Al-Qur'an, 17:81).

When Al-Ghazzali returned to Tus after resigning his post at Nishapur, calligraphy was one of his chief interests. In those days calligraphy was of a special significance, because printing of books was not so common in the Seljuq empire. Men of learning, poets and writers had to depend largely upon manuscripts--classical works as well as their own writings. Al-Ghazzali showed special interests and talent in calligraphy which was the main source of his income in the last days of his life, he had, therefore, to labour very hard for the sake of his other dependents. He even provided free guidance to other calligraphists who took the privilege of coming to learn this art from him.

On the 14th Jumad-al-Ukhra (1127 A.D.) he died at Tabaran, a village near Tus and was buried there.

Quoting Imam Ahmad Ghazzali, (the younger brother of Al-Ghazzali, who was also a prolific writer of an established fame) Ibn Jauzi has related the following story about Al-Ghazzali's death:--

He rose up early in the morning on Monday, performed an ablution, and after offering his prayer, asked me to fetch him a shroud, and when it was presented to him, he kissed it, and lying on his back wrapped himself in the shroud like a dead man, he uttered these words and breathed his last, "O my Lord, Thou art the Helper of the afflicted, the Reliever of all distress, the Consoler of the broken hearted. Thou hast called me to Thyself, and I have come to Thee. Extend to me Thy forgiveness and mercy."

During his rich eventful life he proved a voluminous writer and wrote some seventy books in number amongst which some are standard works on Tafsir, Hadith, Ethics, Theology, Philosophy, Logic, Divinity, Mysticism, Metaphysics and other sciences. The most important works are the following:--

(1) *Ihya'ul 'Ulum al-Din* (Revivification of the Science of Religion).

(2) *Kimya-i-Sa'adat* (Alchemy of Happiness).

(3) *Al-Munkidh min al-Dalal* (Saviour from Error).

(4) *Tahafut al-Falasifah* (Collapse of the Philosophers. A treatise designed to refute and destroy the doctrines of Muslim Philosophers).

(5) *Mizan al-'Amal* (a treatise on logic).

(6) *Al-Mankhul* (on Muslim scholasticism or *Kalam*).

(7) *Al-Wajiz* (learning on theology).

(8) *Mihakk al-Nazar* (on logic).

(9) *Mi'yar al-'Ilm* (also on logic).

(10) *Maqasid al-Falasifah* (a treatise on logic, natural sciences, metaphysics etc.).

(11) *Mishkat al-Anwar* (a niche for lights).

(12) *Mikatib al-Ghazzali* (Letters of Al-Ghazzali).

But what has made the Imam immortal in his famous work *Ihya'ul 'Ulum* (Revivification of the Science of Religion), full of the jewels of wisdom and strewn with mystic and philosophical interpretations of life. This mystical work deserves to rank amongst the greatest works on sufism and stands out as a classic in itself. "Muhaddith Zainuddin 'Iraqi is of the opinion that being a scholar of religion, Al-Ghazzali has successfully attempted to condense and sometimes tc explain the teachings of the Holy Qur'an and traditions in thi immortal work, which is next to the Holy Qur'an and tradition is the last practitional book and the truest religion ir existence."

Imam Nawawi commentator on *Sahih Muslim* writes tha "Nothing like this was written before and nothing like this would be produced afterwards." Of this work it has been observed by Shaikh Abu Muhammad Karzoni that "if all the modern libraries of the world containing standard books on science, religion and arts are accidentally destroyed by fire and fortunately the *Ihya'ul 'Ulum* is left, all human knowledge and all sciences could be revived on the basis of the material contained in this book." This book was written in Arabic and was subsequently epitomised in a more popular and abridged form in Persian under the title of *Kimya-i-Sa'adat* (Alchemy of Happiness) and it served as the text for a series of sermons which the author preached during the course of his wanderings and extensive travels in Syria, Palestine, Arabia and Egypt. The material contained in *Ihya'ul 'Ulum* was being continually advertised by Al-Ghazzali's enemies who wanted to mis-represent him for their own selfish ends. They poisoned Sultan Sanjar's mind against him by accusations of heresy, with which they openly charged him saying "All the great heresiarchs of this Ash'arite section have come from Tus. They have unsettled the faith of the people by preaching danger-hidden ideas among them, thereby weakening the foundations of society."

Regarding this dispute between himself and his enemies, most of whom were *mullas* and *maulvis,* Al-Ghazzali has expressed the following opinion in this book. "These Mullas and Maulvis who call themselves religious leaders deceive and exploit the ignorant masses. They amuse themselves with selfish ends that blind their eyes and hearts to life's secrets. They neither understand the law of God, nor comprehend the true intent of veritable religion. They speak evil of one another. One of them slaps the face of another, then kicks him and plucks his bread. Perhaps you have seen some of them who are beyond forty or fifty years of age, with venerable heads and hearts, kneeling in the mosques with a countenance expressive of the most perfect and peaceful piety, while their hearts are swollen with greed."

"Woe to them who move their lips in prayers with pious words while in actual practice they exploit the religious susceptibilities of the followers. The meaning of true religion has departed and the name remained, the substance has vanished, and the shadow has taken its place. He who knows not the truth, pretends to possess it. The truth of religion has been made false and falsehood has been ascribed to it, with the inevitable result that the hypocrites have become scholars." Some of the so-called theologians also held Al-Ghazzali responsible for his objectionable view about Imam Abu Hanifa's works and they adduced some of his remarks included in his book *Al-Mankhul* as a proof of this. In spite of the fact that Al-Ghazzali strongly refuted this malicious charge in *Ihya'ul 'Ulum,* but they insist on levelling this charge.

The *Al-Munqidh min al-Dalal* by Al-Ghazzali is not of a large size. One can take it along when going on a journey and grasp the meaning of each line, meditate upon the aim and purport of life wondering at the insight and courage of the author, who had nine centuries before raised his voice in defence of reason and social justice, and freedom of thought. He sought the truth through sufism which was his last hope.

He carefully studied the writings of the mystics. As he read them, it became clear to him that now he was on the right path. In November, 1905 A.D.. he left Baghdad and wandered forth to Syria, where he found in the *sufi* discipline of prayer and meditation, the peace which his soul desired. Syed Amir 'Ali to whom we owe the best and the fullest life of Al-Ghazzali says in his learned work *The Spirit of Islam* that Al-Ghazzali propounded a scheme of life which he considered formed the true path *(Tariqat)* to the ultimate goal "the attainment of nearness to Al-Mighty God" and final peace in the beautific vision. His enunication about all nature and all existence, being the direct creation of God, Al-Mighty is but an echo of what is told in the Holy Qur'an. He divides creation into two categories, i.e. the vision and the invisible. The visible world *('Alamul Mulk)* is the world of matter and subject to the law of evolution, change and growth. The invisible world imperceptible to human sense, he divides into two sub-categories; first the *'Alamul Jabarut* which stands between pure matter and pure spirit but partakes of the character of the both. The forces of nature belong to this category. His idea of the purely spiritual world (*Al-'alamul Malakut*) form the most interesting part of this theory. The *'Alamul Malakut* is the realm of "Ideas". The human soul belongs to this world.

It comes as a spark from its original home and on the separation from the earthly body, it flies back to the region whence it came. This is the meaning of Qur'anic declaration: "We come from God and unto Him we return". (Al-Qur'an, 2: 156).

Al-Ghazzali believed that the perceptible universe "has no more reality than a shadow cast by the sun."

The real pessimist sees too much of one thing, and the optimist is too likely to see, of perhaps not to see at all. "I cannot trust the evidence of my sense" says he, "the eye sees a shadow and declares it to be without movement; or as a star, and deems it no longer than a piece of gold. If the senses thus deceives may not the mind do likewise?"

"Perhaps our life is a dream full of phantom thoughts which we must take for realities until the awakening comes either in movements of ecstasy or at death."

Al-Ghazzali bases his doctrine on God as the Holy Qur'an declares it, "He began the creation of a man from dust. He then made his progeny from an extract of water held in light estimation, then he made (his body) complete and He breathed into him of His spirit" (Al-Qur'an, 32: 7, 8, 9). According to Al-Ghazzali the real self is connected with the body through the spirit which is subtle vapour-like substance spreading all over the body. There are two hearts, one the centre of the body which keeps up the circulation of the blood, the other, the centre and the source of spiritual activity. Both are called *Qalb* in Arabic. The spiritual *Qalb* possesses the qualities of will power and knowledge and these are manifested by the faculty of *Idrak* or apprehension. The five mental faculties are:--

Takhayyul or imagination, *tafakkur* or reflection, *tadakkur* or recollection, *hafiza* or memory and *hiss-i-mushtarik* or a common sense. Animals though they possess some of these faculties, have no reasoning power which is called *'aql* or the intellect and thus he is distinguished from animals. The intellect is the cause of human progress. If a man enjoys the gift of nature in its perfection, he realizes the ultimate realities and rises to the rank of angels. But if his soul is overcome by passion and lust, his intellectual activity is weakened and gradually he sinks to the level of animals. Life, therefore, is a constant struggle for the candle to keep its flame continuous by burning or for the drop to attain pearl-hood. Man can be properly apprehended as a living force, possessing rights and duties only in the social organism to which he belongs. Unique individuals must constitute a unique society--a society which possesses a well-defined creed and has the capacity to enlarge its limits by example and persuasion. Such society according to Al-Ghazzali is Islam. Hence his ideas on the individual and collective ego are based on the Qur'anic conception of a perfect Muslim individual and the Islamic society. Islam demands loyalty to God, not to thrones. Al-Ghazzali was of the view, as explained by him in some of these letters, that the king is a shadow of God upon Earth in whom all his subjects must take refuge and be protected. The land and every thing which exists over or under it is the property of God and that the position of a man is merely that of a trustee. Although Islam considers private ownership a trust, it does not allow capital to accumulate so as to dominate the real producer of wealth. Islam recognises the worth of the individual, but disciplines the 'haves' to surrender and give away as trustees to the service of 'have nots'. Islam wants to create a new world, where the social rank of a man is not determined by his caste or colour or the amount of dividend he earns but by the kind of life he lives, where the poor tax the rich, where human society is found not on the quality of stomachs but on the quality of spirits. Wealth, reputation and power are alike unsatisfactory when they are attained, alike insufficient to contend the heart of man, which is ever discontented till it has found its rest. Thus it finds in the prospect of immorality and cultivation of ecstasy by autohypnotic methods and feels itself inspired to such an extent that its existence is lost in God. The search for a purely psychological foundation of humanity becomes possible only with the perception that all human life is spiritual in its origin and that the blood relationship which is earth rooted, should be eliminated as a basis of human society. The least example of the Islamic Government is provided by the Holy Prophet himself (peace and blessings of Allah be upon him) in whom all virtues and perfected; the next is illustrated by the rule of the first four successors of the Holy Prophet (peace and blessings of Allah be upon him) the third is that of a prince, who follows the sunnah; and the fourth, if such a single person is not found is the rule of a number of wise and pious men in co-operation and harmony. Explaining things further Al-Ghazzali states that a tyrannical government tries to subjugate a country for its own pleasure and the pleasure of those constituting it, oppressing the people and appropriating the land at its own discretion. He further advises that a government may be kept in order by concord and unity among citizens and dissensions among its enemies. In order to maintain such harmony, equilibrium should be maintained among the different classes of people. He also held the view that the true kings, princes, viziers and *Amirs* are known by three signs: "Their thought is of God, their dwelling is with God and their business is in God".

According to Al-Ghazzali men are classified into:

(1) Those who are sunk in the darkness of the material world;

(2) Those who are above the material world and inclined towards the spiritual purity and are called virtuous and

(3) Those who are divine and perfect.

The same division is found in the Holy Qur'an:

You shall be of three kinds;

(1) The foremost, who are drawn near (to God) in the gardens of bliss;

(2) The companions of good luck or right hand and

(3) The companions of ill-luck or left hand.

Virtue is likeness to God and classified into practical and ntellectual. The aim is to turn from the world to God. By spiritual contemplation, man is elevated to the eternal bliss till he forgets his limited self and sees the ideal beauty in higher-self. It is communion with the Supreme Beauty and is eternal happiness. Practical virtue is good conduct and the intellectual virtue leads man to salvation. The seeker of truth by "intense inwardness" and communion with God can rise by successive stages of exaltation to a state when he can actually have a vision of the Divine Essence. The first step for the motivate is to form the *niyyat* (the resolve and intention) then comes *tauba* (penitence and renunciation). He is now on the forward path, this stage is called *mujahada* (probation or striving). After a prolonged probation the soul presents itself in absolute surrender to God and abandonment of the world and all its vanities and impurities. The next is "the uplifting of the veil". (M. Mukashafa) when the veil which curtained off the unseen is lifted and God becomes revealed to the worshippers, heart; the last stage is the vision *mushahada* when the soul actually stands in the presence of Truth itself. Even in the primary stage, the psychological effort to concentrate all thought on one subject causes the disciple *(murid)* to see visions, hear the voices of angels and prophets and gain guidance from them. Life is a forward assimilative process and its essence is the continual creation of desires and ideals. The human ego has a definite mission on the earth in two main directions. In the first place, it has to struggle with environment and to conquer it. By this conquest it attains freedom and approaches God, Who is the most free individual. In the second place, the ego has to maintain a constant state of tension and thereby attain immortality. By attaining freedom and immortality the ego conquers space on the one hand and sometimes on the other. The ego has to help in the march of humanity by leading to the birth of a higher type of man, namely the superman or the perfect man who is the ideal to which all life aspires. The following factors and forces fortify the human ego or personality:

(1) Love

(2) *Faqr*

(3) Courage

(4) Tolerance

(5) *Kasb-i-halal*

(6) Original and creative activity.

The *sufis* affirm that the knowledge of God is vouchsafed to them by reason, a gift of the Creator. Does not the Holy Qur'an constantly appeal to human reason and human intelligence "to reflect, to consider, to speculate" about God's creation and the mysteries of nature? Had the Qur'an condemned the exercise of reason, would it have exhorted the people to whom it spoke, to look at the marvels of nature and draw their own conclusions whether this wonderful world was a creation of accident, or was brought into existence by an all-pervading spirit "which sleeps in the stone, dreams in the animal, and wakes in the man."

Dr. Allexis Earrel, a Nobel Laureate in Physiology regrets that "despite the marvels of scientific civilization human personality tends to dissolve." He suggests that "Liberation of man from the materialistic creed would transform most of the aspects of our existence." He goes on to assert that by prayer "human-beings seek to augment their finite energy by addressing themselves to the infinite source of all energy, i.e. the in-exhaustible motive-power that spins the universe." Scientists like Sebrodinger. Rhine, Burrts and a host of others regard science as comparatively less important means of access to ultimate reality and suggest that religious insight holds the key to the knowledge of reality.

"The universe" says Sir James Jeans "looks more like a great thought than like a great machine. It was created by a being with a mind and it is a thought in the mind of such a being." "God", said Dr. Whitehead "is the tangible fact at the base of finite existence". "Science without religion" said Einstein "is lame". A contemporary has said not unjustly that in this materialistic age of ours the serious scientific workers are the only profoundly religious people. The religious feeling of a Scientists takes the form of rapturous amazement at the harmony of the natural law, which reveals an intelligence of such superiority that compared with it all the systematic thinking and acting of human beings is an utterly insignificant reflection. Robert Southey believed that "Religion is the one thing needful without it, no one can be truly happy; with it, no one can be entirely miserable; without it this world would be a mystery too dreadful to be borne."

The times of Al-Ghazzali were not favourable for studies. The crusades disturbed even the quiet cloisters of bowling greens of Damascus and Jerusalem produced violent changes in the government and unsettled the minds of the students and yet not with studying these unpromising circumstances, it was in these two cities that Al-Ghazzali got ample opportunities of perfecting his knowledge in various subjects, which is extremely astonishing indeed.

The great *Imam* with the force of his learning and leadership made the Muslims once again confident of their destiny as the chosen people of God. His mysticism did not border on the renunciation of temporal activities. No doubt, he resigned from his post as a Professor in the *Nizamiya* College and also that of the Grand *Mufti* but he did not get divorced from the world itself. Rather he decided to reform the world and make it a better place to live. He discovered that the social and political life of the Muslims had become so stagnated and rotten that a complete overhaul was needed. The pristine Islamic thought was covered with the cobwebs of alien philosophers and it had become necessary to separate truth from falsehood.

The Muslims were to be saved from doubts and deviations, therefore, he launched his scheme for wholesale reform. He needed an ideologically motivated team of devoted workers which he fortunately found in a large number of his disciples like Imam Abu Tahir Ibrahim, Qadi Abu Nasr Ahmed Bin 'Abdullah, Abu Mansur Sa'id bin Muhammad who purified the society on the one hand, and on the other ran the affairs of the state on true Islamic lines. Thus before his death, Al-Ghazzali had already done more than necessary to awaken the sleeping conscience of the Muslims' world, and bring about a pleasant revolution both in the thought and action of the faithful. The exalted idealism which breathes in the teachings of Al-Ghazzali, did not only inspire the actions of his contemporaries but during the century following his death, it also modelled the lines of the noblest men in Islam. Sovereigns like Salahuddin Ayyubi (the Saladin of European history) and heroes like Nuruddin Zangi found in it their guiding star.

There is no doubt that the Muslims of Spain and North Africa had a share in the development of the Medieval European Arts, Science and Philosophy. Nor is there doubt that men of Europe such as Eckhart Thomas Aquinas and Dante among the ancient and Spinoza among the moderns were indebted to Muslim thinkers. In those days mysticism was the common ground where medieval Christianity and Islam touched each other most nearly. The fact is founded in history. In philosophy European thinkers of the medieval period became indebted to Avicenna, Al-Ghazzali, Averroes and other Muslim thinkers, whose works are studied with eagerness in the European and American Universities these days. The benefits conferred by the nobler type of idealistic philosophy are too great to be ignored. The idealism of Averroes developed in Europe the conception of universal Divinity, as a result of which Christian Europe owes its outburst of subjective pantheism and its consequent emancipation from the materialism of a mythological creed to the engrafting of Muslim idealism on the western mind. It was the influence of Averristic writing that attracted the attention of reflecting people to the problem of the connection between the world of matter and mind and revived the conception of all pervading spirit. Had it not been due to the influence of the Arab thinkers and philosophers the Renaissance in Europe might have been delayed for centuries. Before concluding Al-Ghazzali's biographical ketch it may not be out of place here to mention one of his most important doctrines. He believed that Islam's great message is the unity of God and the fraternity of human-beings. It has caused the fusion of races and abolished distinctions of caste and colour. Racial superiority and social rank are foreign to it. It has taught the fraternity in its true sense. All those who adhere to these principles in theory and practice can be called true Muslims, in whatever else they may differ and not agree. It was Al-Ghazzali who elaborated the idea of evolution through the appreciation of beauty which means perfection and good. Things have either reached their maximum perfection or are yet imperfect strivings after perfection. The imperfect naturally seek the help of the perfect to become perfect. This striving is named love in mysticism. The whole universe is moved by the same power of love towards the one Supreme Beauty, the most perfect, the most good. In the human breast there is love--the love of one Supreme Beauty. It is in this aspect of human aspiration that the thoughts of the East and West meet on common grounds, as if the human mind, in longing to reach its original source works on the fundamental and common principle of love. The peculiar features the European and non-European, American and non-American vanish in the admiration and love of one Supreme Beauty. One nation is like all other nations, because the people are made of the same element every where and do not vary except in their exterior appearance which is of no consequence. The West is not higher than the East, nor is the West lower than the East. Rites and creeds count for little with God, Who dwells neither in mosque nor church, nor temple, but in pure heart. All mystics whether in Europe or in Asia or America sing the same song of loving for the beloved. And poets like Sana'i, 'Attar and Jalal-ud-Din Rumi have given fervent expression to that universal Divine love which pervades nature from the lowest type of creation to the highest and their idylls are regarded by many Muslims with a respect only less than that entertained for the Holy Qur'an. Different nations belonging to the different religions of the world appear to be different, but in reality they are one. There may be differences in detail, in languages, in expressions, in descriptions, but in the main principles, all are united, as drops of one ocean or fingers of one hand. All are seekers of Al-Mighty God and the ways leading to Him are many but He is One. Therefore, according to Al-Ghazzali, if one is sincere in his intention, he will find Him. The essentials thing is a complete moral transformation only to be wrought by ardent faith and humble prayer. God says in the Holy Qur'an: "Those who believe (Muslims) and those who are Jews and the Christians and the Sabians, whosoever believes in God and the last day and does good deeds, they shall have their rewards from their Lord and there will be no fear for them, nor they shall grieve." (Al-Qur'an, 2:62) The idea of the good is co-eternal with Divine love. It is the idea of all ideas, itself unmoved but moves all things and all things move towards it. It manifests itself in all ideas. In other words all particulars are derived from their universal and universal from the single idea of the God which should be sought and known. It has also been laid down in another passage of the Holy Qur'an: "Thou wilt find the most vehement of mankind in hostility to those who believe (to be) the Jews and the idolaters. And thou wilt find the nearest of them in affection to those who believe (to be) those who say: Lo! We are Christians. That is because there are among them priests and monks and because they are not proud. When they listen to that which had been revealed unto the messenger thou seest their eyes overflow with tears, because of their cognition of the truth: "They say our Lord, we believe, inscribe us as among the witnesses." (Al-Qur'an, 5: 85, 86) Advising the humanity to hold fast to the cable of Allah, the Holy Qur'an says further, "And hold fast all of you together; to the cable of Allah and do not separate. And remember Allah's favour unto you: how ye were enemies and He made friendship between your nearts so that ye became as brothers by His grace; and how ye were upon the brink of an abyss of fire and He did save you from it. Thus Allah maketh clear His revelations unto you that haply you (ye) may be guided." (Al-Qur'an, 3:103). In other chapter of the same Book it has been painted out on un-mistakable terms that it is to the devotional state of the mind, that the Searchers of the spirit books, "it is not the flesh or the blood of that which ye sacrifice, which is acceptable to God; it is your piety which is acceptable to the Lord" (Al-Qur'an, 22:37) "It is not righteousness", continues the Holy Qur'an "that ye turn your faces in prayer towards the East or the West, but righteousness is of him who believeth in God: Who giveth money for God's sake unto his kith and unto orphans and the needy and the stranger and those who ask and for the redemption of captives, who is constant at prayer and giveth alms and of those, who perform their covenant, whom they have covenanted and who behave themselves patiently in hardship and in times of violence, these are they who are true". (Al-Qur'an, 2:177). If Islamic *Sufism* is to continue to capture the hearts of mankind, its future will have to be based on the true principles of the fatherhood of God and the brotherhood of man--a religious truth which will exercise a profound influence upon the future history of Islamic thought. Islam may lead the whole world, provided the vast moral and philosophical treasure lying hidden in Arabic and Persian is translated, commented upon and explained in English and other important European languages. When we have tried all ways to happiness, there is no such thing to be found but in a mind devoted to love, freedom and disinterestedness or supreme indifference towards the acquisition of material comforts. If Sufism has always been thoroughly absorbing and transmuting in the past, there is no reason why it should not gain adherents in future amongst men of the most opposite views. There is no doubt that if they would carefully read and meditate upon the following passage of the Holy Qur'an, they would be contended with the wholly positive results:--

> "I have breathed into him (man) of My spirit. Verily We have created man and We know what his souls suggests to him, for we are nigher unto him than his jugular vein." (Al-Qur'an, 50: 16)

ABDUL QAIYYUM

(1)

To His Majesty Sultan Sanjar Seljuqi

In the name of Allah, the Merciful, the Compassionate.

May God bless you with the dominion and grant you a kingdom of heaven before which the kingdom of the whole world stands insignificant. The borders of the earthly kingdom cannot extend beyond the East and West. Generally speaking the average life of a man on this planet cannot cross the age limit of a hundred years or so. The kingdom of heaven is so vast that the whole world seems to be dust particle in comparison to it.

May it please your most excellent Majesty, I realise that for an ambitious man it is very hard to lead a pious life. As I find you very honest and careful, I would have you do this out of wisdom and kindness to your self. Our Holy Prophet (peace and blessings of Allah be upon him) has said: "A day spent in administering justice by a God-fearing monarch is equal to sixty years spent by a holy man in devotion and prayers." If you would ponder over the nature of this world, it would appear dreadfully contemptible. Some of the mystics have said: "If this world could be likened to a picture (made of gold) which is instable and frail and the next world could be compared to a pitcher (made of earth) which is unbreakable and ever-lasting, the wise men would certainly prefer the latter to the former.

As a matter of fact the reality is quite otherwise. This world is a pitcher made of earth, while the next is a pitcher made of gold. Would you not condemn the folly in a man who holds that the former is superior to the latter. If you like a good life and fix your dearest hopes on Heaven, a day of your life would be worth sixty years spent by others in worship, and God would certainly open to you sources of happiness to which you are a stranger.

You should know that by now I am fifty-three years old. Forty years of may life have been spent in the various peaceful haunts of famous scholars and learned men under whom I studied, till I was raised to such a rank that people began to know me and understand the change in my ideas. For twenty years I lived in the reign of Royal father who did all what he could to make both Isfahan and Baghdad the most flourishing cities of the world. On several occasions I served as an ambassador on behalf of your father to the court of the 'Abbasid caliph Muqtadar Billah and did all that was possible to remove certain misconceptions between the Seljuq Empire and the 'Abbasid Caliphate. I am an author of seventy books. For several years I lived and preached at Mecca and Jerusalem, and when I visited the tomb of the Prophet Ibrahim at Jerusalem (peace be upon him) and offered *fatiha* at his *mazar*, I solemnly pledged that:

(1) I shall neither attend the court of a king, nor receive anything of the nature of an emolument from the Governments in any shape whatsoever, since such circumstances would lessen the worth of any services to the people.

(2) I will not get myself entangled in anything which provokes religious controversies. For the last twelve years I have been solemnly faithful to the pledge I made at the tomb of Hadrat Ibrahim (peace be upon him). Now I have received an urgent message from your Majesty asking me to attend your court. In compliance with your orders, therefore, I have journeyed to Mashhad Rada en-route to the capital, but as an after-thought and in view of the aforesaid religious pledge to which I have bound myself, I have made up my mind to cancel the proposed visit. Only I beseech your Majesty to consider the right I have in fulfilling a religious pledge and that I may not suffer only because I have been honest.

If I may undertake to counsel, I think you shall do well to refrain from forcing me to attend your court, nor could you like it in me if I do attend in violation of the pledge. It would make me unworthy of your esteem. And now in my last words I humbly beseech your Majesty to be pleased to allow me to return to my native town Tus, for which act of extreme kindness God will reward you with inexhaustible bounties both here and hereafter, and raise you in the next world to the rank of Sulaiman the great, who was a prophet as well as a famed king.

Your Majesty's humble servant,

Al-Ghazzali.

(2)

To His Excellency Nizamuddin Fakhrul Mulk

In the name of Allah, the Merciful, the Compassionate.

Be it known that the flattering titles conferred on men are a devilish invention and as such are improper for a pious Muslim to accept. Our Holy Prophet has said:

"I as well as the humble and God-fearing men of my community hate the titles and high-sounding appellations." It is very important, therefore, that one must know the real meaning lying hidden in the word '*Amir*'. One who has the virtues of a true '*Amir*' both inwardly and outwardly is an *Amir* even if the people do not call him as such and the one who lacks these qualities is no an *Amir,* even though the entire world may call him an *Amir*. According to the strict letter of Islam, the *Amir* is the one who rules with absolute authority over his lusts and passions. The forces under his command belong to the various categories as laid down in the Holy Qur'an:--

"And none knoweth the hosts of thy Lord but He." (Al Qur'an), 74:31) There are three chiefs responsible for the discipline and maintenance of these forces one is lust which misdirects one to unhealthy and immoral activities--the second is anger which incites a man to murder and the third is greed involving dishonesty and corruption. If these chiefs could be presented in a material form, the first would assume the form of a pig, the second that of a dog and the third one that of a devil.

Mankind is divided into two classes. The first one consists of those who control these three chiefs forcing them to surrender to their will. Such men are kings and *Amirs* though they appear in rags to the naked eye. The second category consists of those persons who cannot but obey and surrender to the will of these three masters. They are obstinate fools who call the slaves of the passions and lust as kings, *Amir* and viziers. They would mislead you to believe that the light is darkness, a thorn a rose and a howling desert a garden: They doubt the integrity of one who holds that this world is a fast fading shadow and that the creation is divided into two categories viz. the visible and invisible. The visible world (*'Alam-i-Sura*) is the world of matter and is subject to the law of evolution to change and growth. The invisible world (*'Alamul-Malakut*) is the spiritual world. The human soul belongs to this world whatever we see in the visible world is nothing in reality though one perceives its existence. Different is the case of the spiritual world. The senses cannot perceive it to exist whereas it does exist. The true believer sees with his spiritual discernment that which the surface investigator cannot see with ocular vision and he understands through his insight that which the superficial observer fails to catch a glimpse. Man sees the true state of things at the time of his death, when the veil is lifted up and the world looks like something turned upside down. What appeared "to be" a moment ago vanishes in an instant and what does not appear "to be" takes a permanent shape and makes itself felt. Placed in such strange surroundings man would shout "O my Lord! How I marvel at what I see!" A Divine voice will cry: "Thou wast in heedlessness of this. Now We have removed from thee they covering; and piercing is thy sight this day." (Al-Qur'an, 50: 22)

Man would pray:

"Our Lord! We have now seen and heard, so send us back: we will do right, now we are sure" (Al-Qur'an, 32:12) and the voice would reply:

"Did not We grant you a life long enough for him to be mindful who would mind? And the warner acme unto you. Now taste (the flavour of your deeds) for evil-doers have no helper." (Al-Qur'an, 35:37)

Again a Divine voice would address him thus:

"As for those who disbelieve, their deeds are as a mirage in a desert. The thirsty one supposeth it to be water till he cometh unto it and findeth it naught, and findeth in the place there of Allah, who payeth him his due." (Al-Qur'an, 24: 39).

Of course it is very difficult for every ignorant and idle specimen of humanity to understand these things properly, therefore, I shall endeavour to make them easy of comprehension by giving them an example. You must have seen the wonderful performance of whirlwind which is a mass of air moving rapidly round and round in a cylindrical or tunnel shape till it reaches a great height.

You think that it is the visible particles of the dust that have set the whirlwind into motion. You cannot see the invisible wind which is the real mover and hence you err in forming your opinion. In this example, the wind is being based on not being and the particles of the dust are "not being" based on "being".

A better example culled from man's body and soul would further explain things to the satisfaction of the intelligent readers. The soul is "being" based on "not being", since nobody can exercise control over it, and every body is placed under its control. Obviously the human body is "not being" based on "being". It is the soul that causes the body to move and act. We can see the thing moving, but not the mover. The sensible world is a shadow and an imperfect image of the intelligible mind and worldly virtue and vice are stages in the development of the soul in attaining harmony, entangled as it is in the world. If you care to think more deeply, you will arrive at the conclusion that in all things He had wonder which shows that He is One. Let us go a step further and we find that this very fact can be explained more appropriately by giving the example of Sustainer of universe Whose Presence is reflected in every particle, but He is Invisible. As all separate intelligence, so all individual souls are embraced by the universal soul. They are all same, because all are offshoots of the same universal soul, yet distinct in individuals. Bodies are formed by nature, the world-spirit which through energy is the direct cause of shape, bulk quantity and quality of matter. Nature is the sum-total of all energies in the world and assumes various forms made active by the reflection of the Real. The soul is not in the body but the body is in the soul. Man's real ego is pure, without motion or consciousness of the worldly objects never separated from its higher self and remains a faded form of the universal Soul. The Supreme Being, formless, attributeless, above goodness, above life, above thought, motionless, neither increasing nor decreasing is yet the true source of all existence. He shines everywhere and every thing is the reflection of Him. The distinction is caused by the successive stages of reflection and every lower state is comparatively a weak reflection turning to its higher for illumination. There is a divine ground in the human soul through which there can be a birth into newness of life and a direct partaking of Eternity. The spiritual goal of life is the feeling of indwelling of God in man, in the unseen depths of his spirit, where he sinks himself into the Divine Abyss. When God finds a person simply and nakedly turned toward Him, He bends down in the depths of pure soul and draws him up into His own uncreated essence so that the spirit becomes one with Him who is above vision and knowledge. It is an inner living love which brings the soul back to its true sources and into union with God Who Himself is love. Such things as the theory of emanation, ascetic life contemplation, ecstasy, devotion, vanity of all earthly pleasures are meant for the men of pure habits, possessed of a religious and speculative turn of mind, but they could not make themselves understood by the illiterate masses. Men of pure habits know their own true worth and reason is their light and their beacon of truth, so that by its light they do not only worship God but also see themselves in their weakness and strength. Blessed are they upon whom He has conferred the blessings of Reason. A number of nations have perished because He did not give them knowledge and they were involved in throat-cut competition which eventually led them to their destruction. Men are classified into:--

(1) Those who are ignorant and have no freedom of thought and speech,, they are chained by customs and traditions and do not know how to follow the light of their own minds or the dictates of their own conscience. These people will attain eternal salvation, thought their ranks will not be high.

(2) Those who are wise, above the material world and are

called virtuous. They are some few and live in every age. They are saved by faith and are guided by ever helping grace.

(3) Those who know not the truth and pretend to possess it, those who have the truth much upon their tongues, but deny it with their acts. They want to secure a high place in this world with pretence of piety and holiness. Such wretched people who follow the dictates of world pleasures will eventually perish and seal their doom in the next world. An example will explain my point. Suppose a patient is suffering from a serious disease and his health hangs upon the choice of an expert doctor, but instead of a specialist, he turn for his cure to a physician who neither understands the nature of his disorder nor knows how to prescribe a suitable prescription, though apparently he professes to be an authority on medicine. Do you think that such a doctor would not kill his patient? People who belong to the third category can be safely compared to such doctors who are devils in disguise. Armed with pretention and hypocrisy they kill innocent persons. The devil himself was one of such doctors, who declared on the authority of a little knowledge which he possessed:--

"I am better than Adam. Thou created me of fire, while him Thou didst create of clay." (Al-Qur'an, 7: 12).

Those who are lost in the passions and lusts of the worldly life and rebel against the will of God are the disciples of an successions to the Devil. God says in the Holy Qur'an:--

"Lo as for My slaves, thou hast no power over any of the them." (Al-Qur'an, 15: 42).

Those who indulge in the variety of amusements that the world makes available and waste their life by doing sinful acts are the disciples of and successors of the Devil. God says:--

"Lo! the devil is an enemy for you so treat him as enemy. He only summoneth his faction to be owners of the blazing fire" (Al-Qur'an 35:6). I most humbly beseech you, sir, to put in your best efforts in following the dictates of the Almighty God and severing your relations with men who are taken to worldly lusts and vanities, for perfect detachment from gods involves perfect attachment to God; in mystical language it implies union with God through love. This is the doctrine that inspires all religious and ethical *sufism*. If you tread the path of *sufism*, it will give a new turn to your whole life and lead you to the regions of eternal happiness. By spiritual contemplation you will be elevated to the eternal bliss till you will forget your limited self and see the ideal Beauty in higher self.

I, therefore, exhort you to live the ascetic life and fear God and lay upon a store of good works against the day of Reckoning. If you find any difficulty in understanding mysticism, read my book *Kimiya-i-Sa'adat* which will direct you to the right path and give you at least a fair chance of making use of the talents with which God has endowed you. Besides, you should also learn the rules of discipline and devotion from a spiritual guide whose guidance you should accept ungrudgingly and seek refuge with Allah Who will certainly save you from the evil of the devil.

Your Excellency's humble servant,
Al-Ghazzali.

(3)

To His Excellency Nizamuddin Fakhrul Mulk

In the name of Allah, the Beneficent, the Merciful

May God keep you alive and make it possible for you to free yourself from your own worldly entanglements. Allah has said:

"You should not forget your own share in the worldly wealth" (Al-Qur'an, 28: 77). This means that you should lay upon a store of good works against the day of Reckoning, because all men are travellers who have to perform their journey through a valley where they have to stagger and slip and where at every step there are so many dangers. How I marvel at those pilgrims en-route to the Ka'ba staying at Baghdad and amusing themselves with wine and sinful objects of extravagance. This will not take them to Ka'ba, where they want to go, but instead of that, lead to endless suffering and misery. The fear of God is the least store that one could lay up against the day of Reckoning, and it is based upon the following:--

(1) Respecting and following the dictates of God;

(2) Being kind to humanity.

Grave consequences would not follow if a king entrusts the office of a minister or that of an executive officer to an inefficient person, but it would be disastrous if he appoints an undesirable man against a post relating to judiciary, since an executive job or ministership is intended to run the affairs of worldly institutions, while on the contrary judiciary is expected to perform the duties delegated by our Prophet Muhammad (peace and blessings of Allah be upon him). The judges are required to arrive at their decisions in accordance with what God has commanded.

"He should judge, according to Allah's notion of justice, revealed in the Holy Qur'an." If you do not want to depart from that affection and the true respect that you should ever bear to the Holy Prophet (peace and blessings of Allah be upon him) and wish to serve the Muslims with a sincere heart, you will raise only such person to the rank of a judge, as is famous for his sense of responsibility, integrity and piety. As we know the prophetic way of approaching things is quite different from that of the executive that does not mean much for mankind at large in the next world. One of the main duties of a judge is to look after the properties of orphans. If he is unjust and does not fear God he would entrust their properties to the custody of dishonest and wicked persons with the consequences of the most fatal kind. God says:

"Lo! Those who devour the wealth of orphans wrongly, they do but swallow fire into their bellies and they will be exposed to blazing flame." (Al-Qur'an, 4:9)

If a judge does not perform his duties honestly in respect of orphans, how could he be expected to administer justice properly in respect of other persons. The case is quite different with honest and pious judges who through their sound decisions, console the down-hearted and shelter the poor and oppressed, who are being crushed under the injustices and evils of the State officials.

I must not forget that I have a favour to ask. A poor old friend of mine who is also known to you and for whom I have a very high regard has fallen upon very hard times. I would like to convey to you the estimation in which the people of Jurjan hold him for his distinguished talents and the usefulness and importance of his learning and piety. These days he is dreadfully distressed as he is too poor to support his large family. Now I want to secure for him that trifling assistance which may enable him to earn his livelihood, and save him from all the sorrow that can be avoided. How this is to be managed, your Excellency best knows. The future is in God's hands.

Your Excellency's humble servant,

Al-Ghazzali

(4)

To His Excellency Nizamuddin Fakhrul Mulk

In the name of Allah, the Beneficent, the Merciful.

I have already told you in one of my previous letters that according to the saying of the Holy Prophet (peace and blessings of Allah be upon him) flattering titles are hated by the pious Muslims:-

"I as well as the humble and God-fearing men of my community have nothing to do with pomp and power". Some people give the name of title to their lusts and all senseless customs as love and regard. Those who cling fanatically to the titles rapidly lost touch with the inner spirit and life which make religion a reality. When a man reaches the height of his splendour, it is immaterial to praise him or not. If someone calls Imam Shafi'i as Khawaja Imam Shafi'i or Imam Abu Hanifa as Khawaja Imam Abu Hanifa, he can be safely accused of trying to advertise those who do not stand in need of advertisement. It is sufficient for all practical purposes to call the Sun the Sun, without prefixing the world "Shining", which is superfluous. Similarly in worldly affairs your Excellency is so exalted that the greatest praise can affect you little. Now let me turn to the affairs of religion which are certainly more important than those connected with this world. You do not think of religion or the next world, which is a pity indeed. I am afraid that you would be condemned to endless misery hereafter, while my wish is that you were in a better world where peace is permanent and there is neither change nor evil. God says:--

"Their reckoning draweth nigh for mankind, while they turn away in heedlessness." (Al-Qur'an, 21:1).

In times of emergency every state seeks protection in its

impregnable fortresses when attacked by an enemy. Some politicians are of the opinion that magnificent horses and beautiful carriages and glittering coffers of gold can overpower the aggressors and that the land forces adequately armed with swords and guns are the best defending forces while other hold that only the states with material resources that have built expensive and majestic fortresses can successfully meet foreign aggression.

The third group maintains that it is only through devout prayer that a nation can escape disaster. And there is no doubt that the belief of the third group is the soundest, because we know that true safety lies in a deep sense of religious devotion and that the Lord does not withhold protection from men, if they steadfastly trust in His mercy and pray for His grace. Others might fall in the hard crisis but the *fakirs* with their prayers must not fall. If they work perfectly in accordance with the Planning Will of the All Powerful Lord, they would acquire immense power. It may all sound absurd to those who suppose that strength and power are to be found only in great armies and equipment or in scientific achievements or in the vastness of economic resources, but as Islamic history reveals that their *fakirs* who did almost nothing but made their souls stainless mirrors for God, nothing but yearn upward into fellowship with Him, they made the most effective contribution to the defence of their country against foreign aggression. It is not the might of the armed forces that save a nation from destruction, it is the humble and ardent devotion of a pure heart that can completely liquidate the forces of darkness of all forms and build a new independent and prospering Islamic state. You should take a warning from the tragic fall of *'Amir of Tus*. It must have made it plain to you that the expensive robes and glittering coffers of gold and silver could not avoid the doom that overlooked them. Instead the material contact of his soul was not a gain but a loss, not an assent but a descent, not a rise but a fall. This has been explained in the following verses of the Holy Qur'an:

> "Woe unto every slandering traducer, who hath gathered wealth (of this world) and arranged it. He thinketh that his wealth will render him immortal. Nay, but verily he

> will be consigned to the consuming one. Ah, what will convey unto thee what the consuming one is. (It is) the fire of Allah, kindled which leapeth up over the hearts (of men). Lo! It is closed in on them in outstretched columns." (104: 2 to 9).

God says further that the hoarders of wealth will cry on the day of Resurrection:--

"My wealth hath not availed me, my power hath gone from me." (111:2).

If you would take into account the suffering to which 'Amir of Khurasan was subjected you would be forced to the conclusion that a bowl containing soup and a loaf of bread in possession of a *dervaish* can work out a miracle which cannot be performed by millions of gold coins or trained soldiers, adequately equipped with deadly weapons, for God is a fortress and castle for all who seek His help. The prayer of a *dervaish* nullifies the effects of swords and guns and unveils the truth that the best fighting forces can safely be recruited from among the people who are observers of *salat* (prayers), fasts and night vigils and who weep during their prayers with the fervour of their emotions. The Holy Prophet (peace of Allah be upon him) has said: "Prayers rid mankind of its suffering."

In another place he has also said:

"Prayer and calamity struggle with each other." I have a written document at my disposal to convince me that your illustrious father, being given to understand that the king of Kirman bore a reputation for his almsgiving and for his feeding the poor, was down-hearted and deeply grieved, not because he disliked almsgiving, but because he wished that no man upon earth should equal or exceed him in good works. You are able to comprehend the powers of your father's mind and you have for it all that veneration which it is both natural and proper that you should feel. Jealously is forbidden except in religious matters. The Holy Prophet has said:

"If envy were proper, two persons would be the most proper objects of it, one a man to whom God hath given riches and appointed to bestow in charity; the other to whom God hath granted the knowledge of religion and who acteth thereon himself, instructing others." Let me tell you that this city was a howling wilderness due to famine and cruelty meted out to the inhabitants by all government officials. Law and order were not disturbed as long as you personally looked after the welfare of the residents of Asfrain and Wamighan. The farmers disposed off the surplus food grains and the cruel officials threatened the oppressed classes, lest they would lodge a complaint with you against them, but the moment you left these two cities, security for persons and their properties have disappeared. The farmers have against resorted to hoarding the grains. If someone twists these facts and misinterprets the actual situation to you, believe me he is your enemy and not a friend. Properly look after your objects. God has given you knowledge so that by its light you may not only worship Him, but also see yourself in your weakness and strength. Each day look into your conscience and amend your faults; if you fail in this duty, you will be untrue to the Knowledge and Reason that are within you. Keep a watchful eye on yourself, as if you were your own enemy; for you cannot learn to govern others, unless you first learn to govern your own passions, and obey the dictates of your conscience.

You should be merciful to your subjects and God would be merciful to you. Do not forget that the residents of Tus are widely known for the miraculous powers of their prayers--the ones whom they adore are blessed and the ones whom they curse are ruined. Several times I undertook to counsel Amir of Khurasan, but he was head-strong, violent and perilously disposed to justify whatever he wished to do with the result that his life has become pages of history for others to take lesson from. You should know that Islam does not allow capital to accumulate in the hands of an individual. Those who agree to part with or spend their wealth expose themselves to a torture which is of three kinds. The first consists in giving away the entire wealth to the needy and the oppressed. Those who do this are blessed by God, for thought it causes them suffering to part with their wealth, yet this contributes to the general welfare of the society. The second class of men are those who spend money in order to defend themselves against vice. These two classes of men attain salvation but the third group of men who live a vicious life and think of nothing else but how to secure a high position in society, are the most wretched people, for they do not think that wealth has always deserted those who fell madly in love with it. They are engrossed in pleasures, vices and sins till death walks silently and slowly towards them, takes their hands, removes their reality and gives to the angels the heavy task of correction.

This is the most dreadful of all conceivable punishments. The Holy Prophet has said:--

"By suffering in this world, man is exempted from punishment in the next."

I have renounced all pomp and worldly pleasures and have severed my relations with kings, viziers and *Amirs*. That is why to the best of my powers I have enforced good opinions on all occasions upon those subjects which are most important to mankind. You should learn how to value my advice and act upon it, however painful sometimes it may be. There are certain men who hate me and try to discredit me with the public. It is easy for them to twist or misrepresent the nature of my writings but I am fully devoted to the great cause for which I stand, and thought my enemies were to scorn and neglect me I should bear their contempt with calmness.

In the name of Al-Mighty Allah and your illustrious father, I earnestly beseech you, sir, to leave your bed at midnight, when all mankind is asleep, wear clean clothes, perform ablution and offer the following prayer, weeping with fervour of your emotions.

"O Lord! I pray Thee or protect me against that vice which Thou knowest."

Creator of all, All-Wise Sovereign Mighty! Assist me in remembering Thee and being devoutly grateful to Thee, for what I am and what I hope to be. Sovereign of the earth, Whose kingdom is ever-lasting and Whose sovereignty is abiding! Be merciful to the king whose kingdom is upon the brink of the most dreadful of all conceivable dooms. Wake him up from the sleep of heedlessness and enable him to work honestly and with zeal for the common man, both morally and economically. My years are darkened by anxieties as to the future of the Seljuq Empire. Thou art the Helper of the afflicted, the Reliever of all distress. Relieve me of my anxieties. If You do not extend Your mercy to the sincere like myself, there would be no other support for a broken spirit; no other balm for a wounded heart".

Meditate on possibilities for an hour or two and think deeply upon the poor people, whose blood and sweat is being consumed by the Government officials. A few moments later you will see how the secrets of God would be all opened to you and your prayers would be heard and answered.

Your Excellency's humble servant,
Al-Ghazzali.

(5)

To His Excellency Nizamuddin Fakhrul Mulk

In the name of Allah, the Beneficient, the Merciful.

May God drive out infirmities and languors from your soul and body and raise you to sublime heights never touched before, so that He may give you what you should desire, a clear spiritual perception of His grace and beauty, as explained in the Holy Qur'an:--

> "And whomsoever it is Allah's Will to guide, He opens his heart for Al-Islam and he whose heart Allah has opened for Al-Islam he followeth a light from his Lord". (6: 126).

When a man is blessed with such in inspiration and illumination, he finds that the people of the world run after material objects and are caught up in a dense and baffling jungle of wild passions, low desires, and aspirations of the animal-self. He takes to renunciation and has nothing to long for. He has no worldly ambitions for he believes that so long as there are desires in the heart, it cannot be cleaned and purified. When all things other than God are effaced and removed from the heart, then alone, the objective is achieved. Begin to search and dig in your own field for this pearl of spiritual glory that lies hidden in it. It cannot cost you too much, nor can you buy it too dear, and when you have found it, you will know that all which you have sold or given away for it is a mere nothing, as a bubble upon the water. People consign their dead parents to the grave and yet they do not take lesson from the incidents, and feel as if they are immortal. They indulge in unlawful things and get out of the law and join the company of the devils who are the enemies of God. So if death overtakes them before repentance, they would be certainly among the losers. On the other hand, a good man believes that death hangs every moment over his head and so he lives such a pious life that he is always ready for death and departs contentedly as he is summoned by Allah, perfectly reconciling himself to his lot. He thinks of those whom he has himself known distracting themselves about idle things, neglecting to do what was in accordance with their proper constitution. All of them have passed away and became a mortal and complete oblivion has buried them. He remembers continually how may tyrants who have used their power over men's lives with terrible insolence, became lifeless packs of decaying elements. What kind of people are those whom men wish to please and for what purpose and by what kind of acts?

How soon will time cover all things and how many it has covered already? How many, after being celebrated by fame, have been given up to oblivion, and how many who have celebrated the fame of others, have been dead. Short lived are both the praiser and the praised and the remember and the remembered as explained in the Qur'an:--

> "Hast thou then seen, if We afford them opportunity (for) long years, And then cometh that which they were promised (How) that whereby they have derived benefit, would not availeth them".
>
> (26:205)

Read the table of your heart and remember what happened to the viziers like Nizamul Mulk and Tajul Mulk, who are now in the next world. These viziers saw with their own eyes and dreadful fall of their predecessors and yet they did not take the warning. They knew that death must overtake them, but they made no preparations for it. They did not think over the transitoriness of the world and want of judgement in those who pretended to give praise and the narrowness of the space within which it was circumscribed and now where are they? No where. God says:-

> "Is it not a guidance for them (to know) how many of generations We destroyed before them amid whose dwellings they walk? Lo! Therein verily are signs for men of thought". (20: 128).

He also says:

"Destroyed We not the former folk, then caused the latter folk to follow after. In this way We deal with the evildoers". (77: 16, 17).

Why then do you choose to act in the same way as these viziers did and why do you not leave those agitations, which are foreign to your constitution? Look within. Within is the fountain of good and it will ever bubble up, if you will ever dig. Remember, if God makes the end to shine for you in the light of His grace, you will abandon yourself utterly to God and devote your entire energy to His service by adhering to the principles of justice and equity. The observance of "Equity" means to dedicate oneself to religion in order to become an enlightened servant of God, guided endowed, illuminated and sent forth as a guide to others whereas justice means to be just to all the servants of Allah. A state cannot make progress, would indeed be subject to disintegration -- unless internally administered among all persons. Islam provides a system by which injustice might be detailed and judged, whether perpetrated by rich or poor, high or low.

When you are required to administer justice on behalf of the Sultan, think as if being an ordinary citizen, you have been oppressed by some one and you want the Sultan to redress your grievances and give you your due. Consider yourself no more than any other citizen. In every thing which happens hold fast to the ruling principles of justice and equity and always keep before your eyes those three things: Objective thinking, acts conducive to social welfare and truthfulness. Do not forget that one who acts unjustly acts impiously. Be ever watchful over the things which are necessary for the administration of the empire. Every moment think steadily as a true believer to do what you have in hand with perfect and simple dignity and feeling of affection and justice and free your mind from all other thoughts. A man's true greatness lies in the consciousness of an honest purpose in life, founded on a just estimate of himself and every thing else, on frequent self-examination and a steady obedience to the will of Allah. The viziers who have already passed away did not have a readiness to listen to those who had anything to propose for the common weal and did not care to give to every man according to his desires. They relied on life, health and riches and sought to build their houses upon the waves and hoped to find a foundation for them there. Now all traces of these viziers have been obliterated:--

> "The likeness of those who choose other patrons than Allah is as the likeness of the spider when she taketh unto herself a house, and lo! the frailest of all houses in the spider's houses, if they but knew".
>
> (29: 41)

The day is not far off when you will be ashes or a skeleton and either a name, or not even a name. And there is nothing more precious in the world than seclusion. I have carefully avoided the pleasant visits to my friends and correspondence with them.

You do not know with what pleasure I have heard the news of your assumption of the office of the Prime Minister of the Seljuq Empire. That is why I have dropped these few lines by way of congratulating you and warning you against the life of this world which is fraught with hypocrisy, deceitfulness and debased morality. After offering prayers for the state, it is the sacred duty of the *dervaishes* to advise the kings, Sultants and viziers and I am glad to think that by writing this letter I have fulfilled my duty as a theologian and a *dervaish*. A long time has passed since the city of Jurjan was deprived of a learned man with true knowledge of religion and ability to act upon these himself and instructing others. I am gratified to know that Ibrahim Mubarak, a highly learned and enlightened man has come to reside permanently in Jurjan.

Possessed of the Divine knowledge, he is the centre of a powerful religious revival and has left and indelible impression on the society. It is because of the fresh testimony of his own experience to the depth of the soul and the pathway to God, his extra-ordinary power as a preacher and his rare gift of interpreting the deepest truth of life and religion that he is held in the highest esteem by the popular audience of the learned persons. He is a God-taught man enveloped in a radiant divine light, obedient to his heavenly vision and possessed of that inspiring trait of personality which makes his life count for much more than his words. He does not teach out of the books, but out of his own heart's experience and makes it a little easier for ordinary people though his help to live a good life. He has accompanied me for nearly twenty years during my extensive travels through Tus, Nishapur, Baghdad, Syria and the Hejaz, where I taught more than one thousand disciples. I have learnt more from his conversation than any other man ever taught me. His facile tongue has illuminated the whole world and his life conforms perfectly with the truths which he preaches. I believe, if there were only one true friend of God in a country or among a people as Ibrahim Mubarik is, that entire country, or nation if it followed the counsels of such a man, would be preserved from the calamities that are to smite the world. Meantime his own boldness of thought and speech have brought him under suspicion on the part of some of the guardians of Orthodoxy and charges of heretical teaching have been levelled against him, but it is only because of his nobility and piety. Some of the influential but ignorant Mullah, of course, have turned against him and he is scorned and hated, and consequently he has withdrawn into a quite retreat to heal the wounds which the world has inflicted on him. I earnestly entreat and humbly pray that you should take a good care of him and draw him near yourself and lavish your bounties on him, as it is your practice to do with the holy men, for it is out of the mercy of the rich that He favours the poor with bounties. May God protect your kingdom against disturbance and decline and bestow upon you the mysterious gift of mystic perception, not for your own glory only, but for the sake of the whole world also.

Your Excellency's humble servant,

Al-Ghazzali.

(6)

To His Excellency Nizamuddin Fakhrul Mulk

In the name of Allah, the Beneficent, the Merciful.

The Holy Prophet has said that there are some enlightened servants of Allah whom He has blessed with beneficent favours. They are brothers to all the servants of Allah and have nothing to do with the wicked world and whatever they have, they distribute it, out of love of God, amongst the poor and the needy. If they perform their duties honestly and diligently, Al-Mighty God uses them as the organs and instruments for bringing relief to the suffering humanity and they become the transmitting centres of Divine light. There are no words to describe the way in which such persons are made to imbibe some of the qualities of Divine Being. It is true that God has also favoured some of the bad persons with some of His bounties, but the main purpose behind this generosity is that He wants them to cultivate within themselves a profound sense of remorse for their past life and a deep regret that their will has been left free to go wrong. This has been explained in the Holy Qur'an in the following words:

> "And those who deny Our revelations, step by step, We lead them whence they know not. I give them rein (for) lo! My Scheme is strong." (7 : 182, 183). The persons having wealth are of the two types:
>
> "Lo! We have shown him the way, whether he be regretful or disbelieving". (76:3).

The least of his graces in the worldly kingdom which he bestows upon his servants, and the best gratitude which could be offered on this account is to support truth, administer justice, eliminate cruelty and oppression and be kind and merciful to those of the subjects who are humble and poor. God has hinted to this effect in the following verses of the Holy Qur'an:

"O David! Lo! We have set thee as a vicegerent in the earth, therefore, judge aright between mankind, and follow not desire that it beguile thee from the way of Allah".

(38: 26).

The ones whom He strikes with His chastisement and wrath are those who, as they attain to higher and even higher stages of fame, wealth and power, pursue pleasure as good and are very cruel to men. It is laid down in the Holy Qur'an:--

"Destroyed We not the former folk, then caused the latter folk to follow after? In this way We deal with the evil doers".

(77:26)

They are like those who build on the brink of a bank undermined by the corrosive torrent indifferent to their fellow-men and ungratefulness to their Creator eventually forces them to declare (in the words of the Holy Qur'an):--

"I think not that all this will ever perish." (8: 35).

The ones who are finally guided hold their wealth in trust and use it for men's service, they have a whole and undivided love towards all men and do not severe themselves from this spirit of universal love or miss this overflow of Divine love which fills their vessels over brimmingful when God treasures the graceful wisdom in the hearts of His good servants, removing therefrom the thick veils of obscurity and brightens them with the light of understanding of His Holiness, they show an almost insane hostility to the forces of darkness and feel compelled to engage in a ceaseless warfare with their enemies, till no trace of them is left. They rise through their good deeds to the highest plane, and they will experience in the new world, "What no eye has seen, nor ear has heard, which has not occurred to any human mind"-which in fact surpasses understanding and which no explanation suffices to cover.

I am sure, your Excellency will spare no pains to attain such proximity (*qurb*) in the high station and lofty standing in loyalty as I know you have the makings of these virtues in yourself.

Your Excellency's humble servant,

Al-Ghazali.

(7)

To His Excellency Nizamuddin Ahmed bin Ishaq bin 'Ali Ibn Ishaq

In the name of Allah, the Beneficient, the Merciful.

God says: "And each one hath a goal towards which he turneth; so vie with one another in good works". (Al-Qur'an, 2: 148). By these words He means that we should set our own unconventional pattern or honest purpose in life and a steady obedience to the rule which we know to be right. (فاستبقو الخيرات) hints to the same effect, that is we should set the best purpose in life. If true holiness is true mindedness, that is the best purpose of life, which fits the individual best for all his relations as a social being and the wise person who would make the best of himself and the most of life will take good care of this purpose gratifying every sense as well and in as many ways as he can because the highest happiness exists as the only consolation in the deep and habitual feeling of devotion. Those who set the best purpose in life may be divided into three groups: Those who are indifferent to the realities of life are common sort of men. There are others who are wise and live in conformity to nature. The third group of men belong to the category of men are enlightened on the mysteries of Divine affairs, and whose hearts are abode of the secrets of God.

The first group of men look at the world which is a fast-fading shadow, and believe that the pleasures in this world are ever-lasting. Being over-powered by pleasures and receiving the impressions of forms by means of appearances, they become the worshippers of wealth and power. These are they whom the Prophet had in view when he said: "Poor wretched, the slave of money! Poor wretched the slave of gold!" Our Holy Prophet has warned that the two wolves cannot cause more destruction to a herd of sheep than that caused to the Muslims by wealth and power. These foolish persons have failed to guard against the wolves who prey upon innocent folk. The world is a prison and these men of the world are prisoners. How strange that the prisoners should revel in misery? He who prides himself upon this world is lowly; he who is rich is in fact poor and he whose power rests upon it is frail. The Holy Prophet has said: "God will inflict punishment on those who worship wealth and put on costly dress". It is a characteristic of the spirit to hoard wealth and adore the decoration of the exterior in all phenomena. This is a curtain that closes to the heart all the perceptions of the unknown. The second type men, i.e. the wise compare this world with the next, and prefer the latter to the former, the true meaning of the following verse of the Holy Qur'an revealed to them:--

"The Hereafter is better and more lasting".
(87: 17)

Evidently they attain to the higher position by discarding the world by their occupying themselves with the Hereafter, for their ideals lies in the next world, which is higher and more honourable and lasting too. They will be satisfied with what they will get in the next world, yet they are not enlightened on the mysteries of Divine affairs which is a pity indeed. The truly enlightened persons belonging to the third group are those who care not a fig for this world or the next and purge their hearts of every thing except God. They know that the final purpose of man's life is to love and to know and to be united with his Creator God Almighty. They worship God for the sake of God, not for any personal end or reward. They realise that to be pulled by the strings of desire belongs both to wild beasts and to men and that they should not yield to the persuasions of the body. They further believe that whosoever desires the life Hereafter, it is incumbent on him to be indifferent towards this world and whosoever desires, God, it is incumbent on him that he should be indifferent towards the life Hereafter. Thus he should discard his worldly life for the sake of his life Hereafter, and discard his life Hereafter for the sake of his Lord. So he should not try to get any recompense and reward for his love for God. The truth contained in the Qur'anic words:--

> "Allah is better and more lasting" (20: 73)

appeals to him and he knows that:

> "Those who would live in Paradise will get fruit (and the pious would be firmly established) in the abode of Truthfulness near the favour of a Mighty king". (36: 55).

Such persons reach above the summit of heavens and once there, they will barter this experience for nothing the universe holds. To these people the secrets of the Muslims' profession of faith (*Kalimah*) LA ILAHA ILLAL LAH (there is no god but God) are disclosed. To express the Oneness of Allah in practice is to know what it is and to know it, is to practise it. For this reason he who knows it puts it into practice and he who acts in accordance with it knows it. So let your declaration of the unity of Allah be LA ILAHA ILLAL LAH. There are many classes of worshippers: Some worship themselves, others their wealth, some their wives, others their children, others their officers and professions. One must worship something or the other. All these are the worshippers of their self and follow its behests. But the real worshipper is one who does not obey the carnal self (*nafs*) and is always taking it to task. These people subject themselves to the verdict of a balance (*mizan*) and discover whether their scale shall rise or fall. They have their hearts balancing their progress, lest either one of their scales be found lacking, for it is with these two scales that they acquire two wings which they can set out in accordance with righteousness in this world; just as the first group of persons when compared with the second is called common and vulgar folk, in the same manner the second class of men, as compared with the third group is common sort who cannot understand the hidden things revealed to the selected few. As your Excellency invites me to a place of new and un-imaginable possibilities of development, in the like manner I invite your Excellency to the attainment of the elevation of your life and its spiritual progress. When you will thus rise from the platform of the common people, you will be made to plunge in one ocean of favours and kindness and mercy and will be clothed with the robes of light and Divine secrets and rare knowledge Divine. The Holy Prophet said:

"When a man treats you with kindness reciprocate him with a better kindness". Since I am too poor to give you a suitable gift in reward for your generosity, with which you have favoured me, I invite you to spiritual lights so that you may be able to receive Divine gifts and get rid of your biological existence.

May you be able to behold beauty and splendour in your own self and recognise that you are a part of the sublime Divine world endowed even with creative life! In this discovery of self you will be able to enter as pure substance into your real self, turning away from all that is external to what is within. Remember, human mind, in longing to reach into original source works on the one fundamental and common principle of love. All mystics sing the same song of love for the beloved. There may be difference in detail or expression, but in the main principle all are united as drops of one ocean or fingers of one hand.

All are seekers of God and the ways leading to Him from Tus and Baghdad are many, but He is One. If you fail to perform a single religious duty, or sleep soundly at night, or you are found guilty of committing a major sin or if a single man throughout your vast empire is reported to have gone to sleep without food any night, remember God's wrath will descend upon you and you will have to lament your indifference in such matters for the rest of your days. You ought to imagine what are the trials, the troubles, the anxiety and the sorrows of a vizier who has been entrusted to run the affairs of the Islamic state. Now I would like to turn to the affairs of the Nizamiyya College and regret very much my inability to comply with your Excellency's commands directing me to accept the post of a Professor in the said college. You know not how infinitely my happiness has increased by retiring to Tus. I have no other desire but the quietness I enjoy here. If I leave Tus and go to Baghdad, obviously my intention in undertaking the journey would be either to gain worldly wealth and glory or add to the religious achievements. Thank God, I have already renounced worldly pomp and glory. This world has nothing to give me and my heart as well as my hopes are in the next. The glamour of the worldly life around me during the period (that I was a professor and grand Mufti) at the Nizamiyya College accentuated the bitterness of my early tragedy which I cannot forget till my death. Even if the seat of the government of Baghdad, together with its vast properties is shifted to Tus it will not be possible for me to dedicate myself to public affairs. If I accede to your request, you would find that my influence (whatever it may be) over a good part of the public, would be greatly diminished, for every one will say that I have sold myself for the Sultan's service. It is true that there are more chances and facilities in Baghdad for the advancement of knowledge than else where and that the number of disciples to be taught there would also be more than it is in Tus, yet in view of certain preventions both worldly and religious, my services to be rendered in Baghdad in the cause of knowledge, would not counterbalance the great loss which my disciples in Tus will have to suffer. Here there are 150 (one hundred and fifty) students who study under me, and it would be inconvenient for them to leave home and accompany me to Baghdad. It would be unjust on my part to injure their feelings for no fault of theirs. Besides, to leave them in the darkness of ignorance in the hope that a large number of disciples in Baghdad would derive benefit, is contrary to reason and laws of natural justice. An example would explain this. Suppose a man is expected to look after ten orphans. He leaves them uncared for and goes to another place to look after twenty orphans. Do you think his act would be justifiable in doing this? Another thing which you should take into account is this: When I first came to Baghdad at the invitation of your father Nizamul Mulk Shahid, I had no family. Now I have a large family to look after, and my children would never agree to my quitting home and it would be cruel on my part to offend or harm them.

I can live peacefully here in compliance with my children's earnest wishes. Were it not for them, I should wish to be in yonder graveyard. When I visited the tomb of Hadrat Ibrahim (peace be upon him) fifteen years ago, I made a religious pledge (covering the following three things) to which I have been faithful to this day:

(1) That I would not attend a king's court;

(2) That I would not accept any emoluments from the Government;

(3) That I would not get myself entangled into religious controversies.

If I break this pledge for your sake, and accede to your request, I fear I shall long feel the effects of any anxiety which will shake every fibre of mine.

In Baghdad one cannot avoid religious controversies and one has to pay homage to the Caliph and I must in the most explicit and determined manner express my inability to do such things. The most convincing explanation which I could offer in this regard is that I can never agree to accept any emolument from the Government, and, you see, Baghdad does not contain my ancestral property which I could fall upon in hard times. If it should please God soon to take me from this world, my family would have resources in Tus quite sufficient for their maintenance. If I leave Tus at this stage, no one will properly look after my property and the result will be that the agricultural lands belonging to me will yield no harvest at all. I know there are people who would be gratified to accept such offers, but so far as I am concerned, they are unacceptable to me. You should know further that it is the evening of my life and I have to prepare for death and not for a journey to 'Iraq, therefore, I humbly beseech you to accept my explanation and forget my audacity for giving up a professorship for a mystical life. Suppose I die, as soon as I reach Baghdad, would you not select someone else for the professorship in the Nizamiyya College? Think my death has actually taken place.

May God bless your heart with a Divine light and enable you to work for the prosperity of the state and its people.

Your Excellency's humble servant,
Al-Ghazzali.

(8)

To His Excellency Shihab-ul-Islam

In the name of Allah, the Beneficent, the Merciful.

May God preserve you in the high station, protect you against all calamities, enable you to guard yourself against the mischiefs of the Devil and place you above all want or the fear of it, and may your heart be free from trouble. The Holy Prophet has said: "Sadaqa and charity are a remedy of all your ills". Ordinary common folk think that physical ailments can be treated successfully with alms giving, while the prominent among men believe that this refers to spiritual malady. God says: "Their hearts are diseased". (2: 10) The physical discceases and spiritual maladies are as different as earth and heaven. The most common and fatal diseases are those which seize the human heart, for one man out of a thousand suffers from a physical ailment, while on the other hand, one heart out of thousand is really sound. Only those who are blessed with sound hearts can claim freedom from spiritual diseases. When one suffers from a physical malady he has no appetite for articles of food and drink, similarly the health of a heart (or one's spiritual health) depends upon one's remembering and paying homage to God.

"Remembering God is the Divine cure of souls".

(13: 30).

because the Al-Mighty God gives man what he desires most, a clear spiritual perception of His grace and beauty. It is only by remembering God that the human heart enjoys peace aright; life of rest and peace in God is good; a life of pain in patience is still better, but to have peace in a life of pain is best of all. He whose heart is dead, does not develop intimacy with God:

"Surely there is a reminder in this for him who has a heart."

(50: 37)

Everyone does not know the mysterious secrets of human mind, nor can he properly differentiate between food and poison. There is a mystery about spiritual realities which will always remain un-explored.

"God is veiled between a man and his heart." The Holy Prophet has said: "Avoid the company of the dead". "Who are they?" inquired his companions. He answered: "They are the rich".

It is not the worldly riches which count but the treasures of heaven and earth which lie stored in the human heart, the possessor of which does not stand in need of a physician to cure him or his diseases, but he undertakes himself to treat his maladies with success. Sometimes he may consult a specialist, who is superior to him in spiritual powers.

Any attempt at serious discussion of *Tauhid* or "The one Reality as opposed to many" is practically foredoomed to failure; because it involves the impossible task of bringing together two attitudes which are not only diametrically opposed to each other, but have no common basis of discourse, and each of which resolutely closes the door upon any thing like genuine inquiry and examination. One cannot achieve *Tauhid* by simply saying that Allah is One. That such introversion is not an easy thing, that it involves a habit of concentration and attention against which flesh and spirit alike rebel is known to all the mystics who have tried to attain to it.

Mystical unity (*Tauhid*) and the path (*Tariqat*) consist of acquired virtues *(maqamat*) and mystical states (*ahwal*) you will find one of such mystics as have acquired these virtues in the personality of Mr. So and So who is personally known to you. A respectable classical scholar, he is thoroughly conversant with Arabic and Persian and is an ardent student of Mysticism with ideas on the subject that have tinged his whole attitude towards life. There are deeper strata of life in him than any logic of the time could fathom or than he himself could explain. Whatever he says is so full of information, and character and there is such a thorough good nature, kindness and frankness about him that I never felt myself more interested in any man's company. He is one of the finest conversationalist of the time. Certainly he must have visited almost every celebrated conversationalist, in Baghdad. If you would listen to him you would testify on the point. I have the highest respect for this man's moral and intellectual character, and as he is too poor to provide his family with the bare necessities of life, I earnestly wish it were possible to obtain a pension for him, which never could be more properly bestowed. I most humbly beseech your Excellency to make your best endeavours in those good offices that may procure relief for the suffering humanity in order to get that blessed reward and honour to transcendent beyond all this world can bestow.

Yours Excellency's humble servant,

Al-Ghazzali.

(9)

To His Excellency Shihab-ul-Islam

In the name of Allah, the Beneficient, the Merciful.

May God bestow His grace upon you and enable you to surrender yourself in every thing so that He may do His work through you. If it be a blessing, His servants devoted themselves to thanks-giving, and if it be a calamity, they either show patience or try to cultivate patience and alliance with God and make endeavours to earn His pleasure, so that their lives may become harmonious to His Planning Will. There are two kinds of *maqamat* or acquired virtues. One is truth, and the other one is falsehood. One lifts himself upon Him attains truth and the other one who values worldly objects more than Him achieves nothing but falsehood. God says in the Holy Qur'an: "I am the friends of those who remember Me". He further says:

> "And he whose sight is dim to the remembrance of the Beneficient, We assign unto him a devil who becomes his comrade". (43: 206).

"When thou seest, thou wilt see there bliss and high state".

The ones who prefer the friendship of others to that of the Almighty Allah, are mentioned in the following verses of the Holy Qur'an:

> "As for those who disbelieve, their deeds are as a mirage in the desert. The thirsty one supposeth it to be water till he cometh unto it and findeth it naught and findeth in the place thereof Allah, Who payeth him His due, and Allah is swift at reckoning". (24: 39).

As this world is a means for reaching the next, a wise and enlightened person does not make the means an end in itself. He stands condemned who sells the next world for this.

The Caliph 'Umar bin 'Abdul 'Aziz was a practical moralist. Before his coming into power, when a piece of cloth costing one thousand dinars was brought for him he would say: "Alas! It is too coarse for me to wear". But after his coming into power when a dress costing rupees five only was brought for him, he would say, "Alas! It is too fine for me to wear. You do not know how I wish my dress was made of coarse sack-cloth, so that by its touch, the skin of my hand was scratched all over".

People inquired of him of the two opposite attitudes of his mind and he said: "Prior to my accession, my self (*nafs*) had such a refined taste as it could not be satisfied with what it got and strove after better but after my accession, I have been following a rigorous discipline and living such a simple and austere life as the poorest *fakir*. I want a little and I always have the little that I want. There was freedom for him from perturbations with respect to things which came from the external cause and there was justice in the things done by virtues of the internal cause. He ceased to be held by pains and pleasures which are as much inferior as that which is to be served by them is superior, for the former are loose and corrupt and the latter is intelligence and piety. Man is given a limited will. It depends upon him either to identify his being with his selfness, and its interests or throwing aside his selfness, identify himself exclusively with the Divine within and without. This is the path of enlightenment.

God has raised you to the high rank of the premiership of the Seljuq empire. The time has come now when you should wish for a rank higher than this and when you get it and feel satisfied with it, you will be transferred from this stage towards another which is higher than this, and you will be turned towards one which is more honourable and you will be rewarded with a feeling of self-sufficience and the doors of salvation will be opened unto you as explained in the traditions of the Prophet. I have written this letter with a definite purpose of introducing you to one of my old friends. Both his inspiration upon his disciples and his dedication to a noble life are due to intimations from beyond what seems to him to be domain of his own self. He is the father of religious society of a mystical type, the members of which believe that they could be organs of the Divine spirit. He is an old man and too weak to earn his livelihood. His manifold hardships, his arduous labours and the ill-treatment that is meted out to him are quite sufficient to explain the ill-health that he suffers from. Besides, Abu Bakr 'Abdullah, who is said to be so favoured as that the hidden things of Heaven are revealed to him, has asked me to introduce him to you with a request to help him out of his financial difficulties. Of him he has said in his letter addressed to me that, "Whatever may have been his theory of knowledge, there can be little doubt that to him more than to any other mystic that ever lived, we owe the conviction that man's soul is allied with a realm of Eternal Reality and can in a moment travel thither".

I pray to God Almighty to open the doors of His everlasting kingdom unto your soul, so that it may behold all that happens on this earth and may He enable you to renounce your own worldly advancement for the sake of the life Divine which is better.

Your Excellency's humble servant,
Al-Ghazzali.

(10)

To His Excellency Shahab-ul-Islam

In the name of Allah, the Beneficent, the Merciful.

I praise God for the bounties He has conferred on you and thank Him for ridding our Islamic State of the enemies, unholy conspiracies and calamities of time and space. I am glad to know that you have safely returned from your expedition, and congratulate you on meeting your family again. I hope you are fully recovered from the tedium of the journey. It will not be out of place to remind you that your prosperity as well as the welfare of the State depend upon the fervent prayers of the pious who saved you from all dangers both internal and external and lifted you to your present pomp and grandeur. I believe He will accept prayers about you in future also, and raise you to such heights as are beyond the reach of the worldly accidents. This will be possible only when you weed out whims, exercise restraint on the desire, extinguish appetite and keep the love for power well within control. You should entirely dedicate yourself to studies and do every thing possible to promote the cause of religion and trouble yourself about nothing else. Depending upon God in utter humility is one of the first steps on the high way of holiness. One must lose all desires to set himself above others. The soul must sink down into absolute seclusion and become "lost" so that it may be "found". Your real enemy is in yourself and should go to battle with that enemy. True devotional spirt demands that you should be thankful to God in prosperity and resigned to His Will in adversity. God says:

> "Say: In the bounty of Allah and in His mercy, let them rejoice therein. It is better than what they hoard."
>
> (10: 58).

It is a pity that people depend for happiness upon human beings, most of whom disturb the world by doing wrong.

There are those whom God says:

> "The likeness of those who choose other patrons than Allah is the likeness of the spider whom she taketh into herself a house and lo! the frailest of all house is the spider's house, if they but know".
>
> (29: 41)

There is no power or strength except in Allah. When you see one who trusts in men and depends on them relying on them in all his deeds, yet professing a station of loyalty and piety certainly beware of him, for he is a man of conceit and dissension. If you trust more in your Master than in your own fellow-men, then you are loyal to Him and He is your Master indeed. In this age the commoners are involved in various kinds of difficulties and humiliations only on account of their pre-occupations with the world and their attachment to it and their indifference towards the Hereafter and its problems and their unmindfulness of the Day of Judgment. May God keep you in harmony with His commandments and spiritual glories which are more important than any that could be discovered in the world of matter, and may He enable you to perform all the offices and duties which man of God could perform for people in distress. Power of strength lies with God Who is the Beneficient and the Merciful.

Your Excellency's humble servant,

Al-Ghazzali.

(11)

To His Excellency Mujir-ud-Deen

In the name of Allah, the Beneficient, the Merciful.

God says:

> But seek the abode of the Hereafter, in that which Allah hath given thee and neglect not thy portion of the world, and be thou kind even as Allah hath been kind to thee".
> (28: 77)

Your Excellency must mediate upon the secrets of the Divine message contained in these verses, each one of which is the pearl of Divine knowledge. If you are blessed with a spiritual enlightenment, you would be able to cast yourself headlong into this divinely ocean, in order that you yourself may find the pearl that is worth more than all the goods of the earth. You should dig deep for the pearl that was never hidden in any earthly field. He who worships the gods of position and wealth and is overpowered by basic pleasures, is too ignorant to appreciate the true meanings contained in:

"But seek the abode of the Hereafter in that which Allah hath given thee."

God says about him:

> "Whoso desireth the life of the world and its pomp, We shall repay them their deeds herein and therein they will not be wronged. Those are they for whom is naught in the Hereafter save the Fire (All) that they contrive here is vain and (all) that they are won't to do is Fruitless."
> (11: 16)

My God! How strange, the one whose lifetime runs out while he hoards gold. Poor he is with all he has amassed. It is impossible to make known to him the meanings contained in the verse:--

"And neglect not thy portion of the world".
(28: 77)

For the Prophet has explained man's due share in this world, "You possess the right of ownership only in the articles of food which you eat and dispose of, but the money you give away to the poor (by almsgiving) can never be spent, since Allah gives increase manifold to whom He wills".

Those who try to get any recompense and reward for their piety from God, the Mighty, the Glorious, in this world or in the Hereafter in the form of Paradise are not true lovers. Those who have surrendered their will to God, they have undoubtedly nothing to do with Paradise and its comforts. Their only object is nothing but the friends. The only true mystic motive is the love which desires not the gifts of God but God Himself and which cannot rest until it is transformed to the Divine thought. Those who desire the gifts of God, instead of God Himself fail to understand the meaning lying hidden in:

"And be thou kind even as Allah hath been kind to thee". (28: 77)

The Holy Prophet who was asked by Gabriel to explain the meaning of beneficence replied "Worship God, as if you see Him with your own eyes". It is obligatory on the part of the one favoured with Allah's grace that he should be grateful to Him. Subject yourself to the verdict of your conscience and think deeply whether you can attain to a still higher type of Divine grace. If so try by all means to achieve it and do not be satisfied with the portion which has already been given to you. If you are able to receive more through firmness, then you shall be among the owners of stations and ranks. Thus you will attain to higher and even higher stages of Divine grace, till you are enriched with a wealth after conformably which there is no poverty. Hadrat 'Umar b. 'Abdul 'Aziz, by living to this ideal of contentment obtained all that he wished or expected. He was not fond of building houses, nor curious about what he ate, nor about the texture and colour of his clothes. All pride was taken away from him and he had been fully convinced of that it is possible for a man to live in a palace without guards and embroidered clothes, and without torches and such like goods of pomp and show. We have bodies and senses like animals, but we have reason, intelligence and insight which bring one near to God. There are three quite diverse types of men. There is the person who has little or no interest in this world, which is a place of voluptuous and sensual enjoyment, for he believes that man should get rid of the desires of the flesh and cast away his earthly limitations and worldly trappings. Whosoever sets the religious trap of artfulness against the world, shall thereby capture hope for being among those who fear Allah. Though this sort of renunciation is not of the superior type, yet people belonging to the category will achieve salvation. The other type of man has unveiled before him the picture of abstract beauty in which is manifested the splendour of His name, the exalted, that is resplendent in all creation through various phenomena. He, therefore, abandons struggle in the narrow straits of lower regions of this world and rises through his energy to the higher plane. He can never be content with biological existence. That is why he does not respond to the world which his senses report to him, and instead he exclusively confines himself to the other world. Being more responsive to another realm of Beauty, he seems from the first to have come with trailing clouds of glory from God and is aware that he belongs to the father land of the spirit. The third type of man is one who has stripped himself of all property and pleasures, either of this world or the next world, for the sake of his Lord. He understands the logic behind.

"God is Best and Eternal". He maintains that so long as any desire from among the desires of this world and that of the world beyond that continues to disturb his heart in regard to the various things of food and drink and dress and marriage and residence and conveyance and rulership, he is certainly not a pious man because in every one of these things there is a relish and pleasure for the self of man and liking for urges of flesh. The animals share some of these desires and it is humiliating for man to be content with what animals possess, for though man had a body and senses like an animal, yet having reason and intelligence he is superior to animals in all respects. His disinterested love brings him near to God. It is not industry that brings him to the goal. It is finally the grace of God, after he has taken the steps of purgation and preparation which makes his life meaningful in the spiritual sense. Then he stands at the beginning where he can catch the glimpses of the spiritual world. There the Divine kindnesses flow in his veins till he is covered with celestial light till he can sing and rejoice and delight in God, as the angels do, as revealed in Qur'an:

> "But unto Allah belongeth the after (life) and the former. And that thy Lord, He is the goal".
>
> (53: 42).

May God favour you with the rank of the chosen few, who belong to the third type of persons and enable you to meditate upon the meaning of و ان الی ربک المنتهی for the secrets lying hidden in this verse have not been disclosed even to those who are famous for their learnings. I think I should be a little exalted by remembering that you had been once my friend. You do not know how I am filled with gratitude to remember the days when I received kindness from you in Baghdad. I have never forgotten you during my extensive travels through Syria, the Hejaz and 'Iraq, during which period I have always prayed for your long life and prosperity. Now for the past several years I have preferred a life of seclusion and renounced court-life and correspondence with the Sultans and the Amirs. There are two reasons to justify my violation of this principle by writing to you this letter. Firstly, I wanted to meet you, and since it was not possible for me to do so, I thought it were better to contact you through correspondence. The people of Tus join me in extending to you our warm greetings and cordial felicitations on the auspicious occasion of your assumption of the Prime Minister's office. You are held by the common folk as a great vizier of whom they entertain high hopes, admiring your talents and giving you credit for your virtuous desires.

Secondly, many evils have taken root in this part of the country, which could only be weeded out with your careful attention, and I write to you for this purpose.

Mr. So and So who is personally known to you, hearing the good news of your assumption of office, made up his mind to attend your court and congratulate you, as soon as it was possible. Prior to his proposed visit to your goodself, he wished me to advise him if his departure from the city at this stage would be justifiable in view of certain works that required his immediate attention, and I replied in the negative, telling him that he should postpone his visit to a later date, till he is in receipt of your definite instructions.

As a large number of disciples study under him, I think his absence from Tus would keep them off their usual pursuit of knowledge and the city would wear a deserted look till he arrives back. He has served the State sincerely and honestly as a judge in one of the district courts, but some of his influential enemies in the Sultan's court, raising certain false allegations against him have been successful in throwing him out of service. He has to make his living chiefly by his profession as a judge and I am sorely disturbed to find that he, whom I value as one of my dearest friends, should find himself too poor to support his family. Circumstances have forced him to resort to the religious teachers' profession for the time being to earn something that his family should fall upon, but I do not see any reason why he should be deprived of his post for long. He is the most capable judge, devout and orthodox Sunni, harsh towards heretics, especially the Shi'ites and Ismailies, a liberal patron of the men of letters, a sincere friend to men of virtues and learning and unremitting in his efforts to secure public peace and justice and to promote religion and education. Since the Government always stands in need of the services to be rendered by such a judge, I hope your Excellency's announcement will give an indication of your next move towards the reinstatement of the official on his former post so that the people of this part of the country mav pray for you, for the rest of their days.

Tus is a rich and secure city and the peaceful haunt of scholars and learned men. Their prayers serve as a shield against wrong, but the age in which we live is one of the most critical in Islamic history. Party feelings run high and they have led the people into narrow and separate views and suspicions. Some of the prominent men and the so-called theologians of Tus are head strong, violent and perilously disposed to justify whatever they may wish to say. These theologians are objects of envy and jealousy and victims of their selfish desires. I have never felt half so much excitement in political events as the present state of Tus has given me. Party squabbles and the Government's ineffectiveness have opened the door to a wave of social violence which has gripped the country. The judge whom I have referred to (if re-instated) would report to you the underground activities of the mischief-mongers as he is a most reliable person and his knowledge covers every thing that happens in the country.

Now I would like to request you to grant him that trifling assistance, which may enable him to earn his livelihood in reward of which the country would be saved from calamities and people would pray for you.

May God accept the prayers of the Muslims in respect of the Mujir-ud-Deen.

Your Excellency's humble servant

Al-Ghazzali.

(12)

To His Excellency Mujir-ud-Deen

In the name of Allah, the Beneficent, the Merciful.

God says:

> "Respond to the call of your Lord before there cometh unto you from Allah a Day which is no averting. You have no refuge on that Day, nor have ye any (power of) refusal. But if they are averse, We have not sent thee as a wonder over them. Thine is only to convey (the message)". (42: 47).

That which cannot be avoided is death which hangs every moment over the head, and when it comes, you will be sorry, but your sorrow will not benefit you, and you will make excuses, but no excuse will be accepted and you will cry for help, but no help will be forth-coming.

The wise man par excellence is one who by renouncing desires of the flesh does not fall into evil, remain prepared for death every moment and collects goods that shall accompany him on the last journey and you cannot collect goods for your last journey unless you retire unto yourself. For nowhere with more quietness or more freedom from trouble does a man retire than into his own soul, particularly when he has within him such thoughts that by looking into them he is immediately in perfect tranquillity and tranquillity is nothing else than the good odering of the mind, and when he lays aside all carelessness and passionate aversion from the commands of reason and all hypocrisy and self love, he becomes strong enough to serve the suffering humanity. Every town and city in the country has turned into a battlefield where the strong wrestle down the weak and the rich exploit and tyrannize over the poor. Whoever helps such poor people, his title in the heaven would be Mujirud-Daulah. Titles come down from heaven as Jesus Christ once said "Verily, he to whom God hath granted the knowledge of religion and who acteth there on himself, instructing others will attain to a high station Hereafter".

To be just to one's own soul means to be purified of all the inner impurities including low desires: anger, lust, hatred, greed, pride and revenge etc. Take pity on your soul and be kind to it and bring into use all the instruments for the service of your Lord and surrender whatever is to Him. You should show an almost insane hostility to yourself, and ride on your animal self and after disciplining it, traverse on its back the paths of safety. The moment you do this, you will feel the first divine illumination and you will acquire the immediate knowledge of God ,which is the highest thing which a man can attain. The Prophet has said: "Had not the devils misled men, the latter would have held sway over the kingdom of heaven. One who clearing away through the senses, rises past his own mind to the wisdom of God, deserves to be honoured in heaven with the title of Mujirud Daulah. Since you are the wisest of all the viziers who have passed away, I feel sure, you would remember that the attention given to every thing has its proper value and proportion. Do not forget this then that the day is not far off when this little compound of yourself would be dissolved or removed and placed elsewhere. You should fear death and learn to live according to nature.

Take pity on your subjects and be kind to them, for I have reliably learnt that there is no limit to the tyranny exercised by the strong over the weak. A year ago when I saw people who were wasted away by a long anxicty and under whom their limbs trembled, I could not bear the agonizing sight and left Tus consequently, but when urgent private affairs forced me to visit Tus again, I found that the same forces of darkness were still in the ascendent and that the people had become poorer and more oppressed and no body cared to save them from the clutches of the tyrants.

Refrain from torturing the innocent masses or else great will be your disgrace from Allah. If you want to escape this punishment, fight the forces of cruelty and injustice like a spiritual here and do not yield to their behests, for if you purge yourself of selfness and help the cause of God by opposing the enemies of his servants, you will develop friendship towards men and obedience to God which will lead you to the highest rank beyond the reach of the kings of this wicked world. If you want to serve suffering humanity, you will have to realise that it is possible for a man to live without the rich or embroidered dresses which is the mark of pride. Can a common man by wearing the garments of a woman become a female? If that is not possible, how can you by wearing women's garments become like them? He who offends through precious dress, seems to be in a manner more intemperate and more womanish in his offences. Nothing is more wretched than a man who tries to look like a woman. If you think a while, you will know that nobody bothers about you. Should men befriend you, it would only be serving their own ends. Many a people adore you, because as a Prime Minister you are the god of position and wealth. They who are praising you now, will blame you and praise another, as soon as you quit your position and some one else is appointed in your place. When you behold a man who welcomes praise know that he is verily a liar and a potent danger for you. You should provide for the smallest without display and check immediately popular applause and all flatter. The seeker of false prestige among men is a cheat, he shall not be able to impress men and instead he would incur the wrath of his Master. The words which were formally familiar are now antiquated, so also the names of those who were well known in the past, are now in a manner antiquated, for all things soon pass away and become a mere tale and are soon cast in oblivion. And I say this of those who were well-known to the world. For the rest as soon as they have breathed out their breath, they are gone and no man speaks of them. The frailest of the ties is the one based on deceit and pride, it is like writing on water or choosing to go away against the tide:

> "The likeness of those who choose other patrons than Allah is as the likeness of the spider when she taketh unto herself a house, and Lo! The frailest of all houses is the spider's house". (29: 41).

Let there be movement and action terminating in social

justice. As means of living in conformity to nature, we must develop wisdom or the knowledge of good and evil which is one of the chief virtues, each one of which has its proper sphere. He indeed is the wisest who hates the things which constitute worldly life. And he loves the things which contribute to his life in the Hereafter where he is going to remain for ever and gets composure of mind and satisfaction. If all the kings of world want to serve him, he would decline to accept their offer. Those who accept kings in their services, are still the servants of their desires and their happiness and sorrow depend upon others. The Holy Prophet (peace and blessings of Allah be upon him) said to Hadrat 'Ali: "If other people seek salvation through good deeds seek entering into union with them through your knowledge of good and evil". He said this as he knows that the seekers of God are like those who are possessed of the knowledge of Kimia: a precious metal upon the mere touch of which solid things turn into gold and those who seek God through good deeds are like the persons who have some money to support them for a few days. It may be explained that with enlightenment and knowledge, men seek to illumine their surroundings, with the light proceeding from God in the midst of darkness of destiny, and hold fast to the injunctions and prohibitions of God and traverse under the direction provided by the Qur'an and Sunnah, the path towards their Lord. They renounce pleasure, wealth and power of which are the general objects of human ambition that entails suffering. One of their ambitions is to make their souls a stainless mirror of God and to crucify every thing that hinders in coming of divine illumination. It is the peculiar office of the national and intelligent motion to circumscribe itself and never to be overpowered either by the motion of the senses or of the appetites for both are animal, but the intelligent motion claims superiority and does not permit itself to be overpowered by the others. When man is free from the bondage of desires relating to this world and the next he would see God with his own eyes and be united with Him. Those who love God for the sake of Paradise are not among his friends or *auliya'*, for they worship Him not for the sake of pure love, but for His bounties like people who worship kings and viziers for the sake of their favours. As God has blessed you with knowledge and enlightenment I beseech you to seek your Lord through the two channels the Qur'an and Sunnah, so that you may attain to the position to the wisest. Meanwhile I must warn you again against falling into the trap of the mirage of life, where your thirsty soul would find nothing and you would suffer a great deal. Those who respond to the world which their senses report to them and seem to care little about intrinsic values or have little or no interests in things beyond the world of sense are unconscious of the ascendent realities because they are careless and ignorant and their lust overpowers them to seek an extent that they have no time to meditate upon transcendent Realities. There are two reasons for their refraining from traversing the path towards the good of life.

Firstly, they are slaves to their passions and cannot part with wealth and fame they have earned. The best remedy to cure this disorder is that they should love God simply and constantly and accept piety and renunciation as their ultimate goal. The enlightened understand this secret. This world is the abode of misery and suffering and the moment we get rid of our personal relationship with it, God makes the end, so to shine for us in the light of His grace, that even while on earth, we feel as if we sit in heavenly places.

Secondly, they look upon the next world with suspicion and refuse to believe that it really exists. It should be made plain to them that even in the belief of God all men do not agree, though their lives furnish an opportunity to seek peace of mind through God. The most reliable cure for this disease is that the patients should retire into themselves, for it is in their power to do so. This retirement into themselves will send them back to Allah, free from all ideas of pantheism. This type of men, however, are not completely devoid of spiritual capacity but are composed entirely of material stuff. Their unconcern for God or the life Hereafter is due more to the influences of nature and social pressure than to an original bent of mind. They should be told that the soul has an eye as surely as the body has by which we may know the sovereign truth and may learn to love the sovereign goodness which is God. This type of truth can be got from the mystics who have been liberally educated in the science of God. "You should inquire from people possessed of the knowledge of God in matters which you do not know" (16: 43).

Just as a physician knows through his reasoning faculty and experience that man lives upto a certain age and that he eats different foods to keep him in health. He also knows that poison brings death to man. Similarly we know that man is destined to live an eternal life which death cannot take away and that his salvation lies in forgetting all earthly things even himself so that in the enveloping light he may see marvellous things and be filled with divine joy. Salvation is one thing and to be blessed with divine grace quite another. No amount of poetical imagination or religious institution of a very high order could attain to these truths, which cannot be picked up out of books, for the soul may see more in an instant than can be written in the voluminous books. The words are all coined to express things which belong to the realm of space and time and obviously they do not even quite fit a reality which stands in eternity. We see and feel and know imperfectly very few things in the few years that we live and all the knowledge and all the experience of all the human race is positive ignorance of the whole which is infinite. The development of the soul is not something that comes from nature, it derives from the grace of God, without which all works which man can even work to the end of the world are an absolute nothing. The mind's eye of the meditator perceives the vision of the beauty of the presence which at one glance fills his mind to the exclusion of all other objects. This is "tauhid". In view of these spiritual truths I request you to keep a watchful eye over your self each day, and find out the causes which have led you astray and then amend your faults so that if you cannot administer justice in respect of your poor subjects you may at least learn to govern yourself properly and obey the dictates of your conscience.

Your Excellency's humble servant,

Al-Ghazzali.

(13)

To His Excellency Mujir-ud-Deen

In the name of Allah, the Beneficent, the Merciful.

The Holy Prophet has said: "Whosoever is kind to you, reward him with a superior kindness". Truth is always bitter and the one who patiently bears bitter things being said against him, dose not fail of valid spiritual achievement, for he possessed of extra-ordinary self control.

Due to this reason you deserve my whole-hearted prayers and I sincerely hope that God Al-Mighty would enable you to appreciate the value of true blessings which He would set aside solely for you. You should know that the blessed is the one who carefully follows the advice of others. This involves a steady and searching discipline. The first man who was deprived of this blessing was Tajul Mulk. He saw the tragic end of Nizamul Mulk's reign with his own eye, yet he did not take any warning and instead being led, astray by false hopes about himself, said to himself, "Nizamul Mulk was too old to adminisier things efficiently and I am a handsome young man". Soon he was stretched dead and reduced to ashes. Majidul Mulk ought to have taken a lesson, from Tajul Mulk's life, but he too failed as the glamour of fame cheated him and he said to himself: "The well wishers of Nizamul Mulk turned enemies to him and accused him of serious charges including corruption. No body can find fault with me and I have every right to govern the people as I will. His life too is gone. He indeed has not been remembered even for a short time. On his death-bed the angel of death delivered to him the following message of God:

> "Did not We grant you a life long enough for him who reflected to reflect therein? And the warner came unto you." (35: 37).

Then came the turn of Muyid-ul-Mulk. He too was not shaken awake, though he had already seen many, who after mutual enmity, suspicion, hatred and fighting were dead long ago. Like others he also recalled to his mind this conclusion. "The viziers who have already passed away sought power for mean ends, therefore, all hearts were hardened against them and they were deprived of all their desires. I do not belong to the category of such viziers. I will use my country for my own benefit, as I deserve it, being a legal heir to the premiership."

Soon the fate removed him to another sort of life. Now it is the turn of Mujir-ud-Din or Mujirud Daulah, and an affectionate Divine voice addresses him thus:

> "Is it not a guidance for them (to know) how many a generation We destroyed before them, amid whose dwelling they walk? Lo! therein verily are signs for men of thought." (20: 128).

The message meant for you in these verses is : "O, vizier, do not deprive yourself and your family of the good wishes of the wise and the enlightened. The other viziers who are now in the next world had erroneously separated themselves with the devoted prayers of the pious with the inevitable result that a dreadful doom overtook them.

> "How many were the gardens and the watersprings that they left behind. And the corn lands and the goodly sites. And pleasant things wherein they took delight! Even so (it was) and We made it an inheritance for another folk not for them, nor were they reprieved". (44: 25).

Look into yourself and if you spend your life like others, what explanation you will offer:

> "Hast thou then seen, if We content them for (long) years, and then cometh that which they were promised (How) that where-with they were contented naught availeth them"? (26: 205).

I must bring it into your notice that none of the viziers of the by-gone days was as notorious for his bad deeds as you are. The mass of wretchedness and of ruin which your administration has occasioned is beyond all calculation and yet you do not feel pity towards the inhabitants of Tus who have already suffered heavily. Though you would dislike these things being said against you, but the Holy Prophet has said in his traditions that on the Day of Judgment the guilty alone would not be held responsible for their crimes, but their relatives would also be subjected to humiliating punishment. You must realise that no one is concerned or worried about you, therefore, you should feel pity towards yourself, avoid too much social contact with men and dedicate yourself to good deeds so that you may earn peace of mind in this world as well as in the next. To attain the Divine grace that is the ultimate hope for man's salvation, you should make your memory a tablet on which the actions of the deceased Viziers like Nizamul Mulk, Tajul Mulk, Mujeerul Mulk and Muyidul Mulk are inscribed. Carefully read these inscriptions and then you would be able to turn away from worldly traps and vanities. If you cannot get rid of these vanities as it is too late now to do so, collect good for the journey to the next world and no good is superior to your efforts you make for the climmation of poverty and cruelty at the hands of which the poor people are suffering. As soon as possible and so far as it lies within your power you should spare no pains to ensure that corruption, nepotism, injustice, bribery, cruelty and other ills are completely wiped out. The people are the glory of our kingdom and the source of its wealth. You do not know the present state of their finance. You can have no idea of an anarchy that exists in this part of the country. The corrupt revenue officials exploit the ignorant masses for their own profit and do not credit the amount of taxes and other Government dues (charged at exorbitant rates) into the Government treasury. Think upon your subjects, broken in body and groaning under poverty and of hunger. Their limbs tremble under them. Long anxiety has reduced them to a skeleton, while you are leading a life of luxury and indifference. If any thing can ruin Khurasan and 'Iraq too, it would be because of such ministers who have been made the incharge of affairs.

Don't let any feeling of pride withhold you from acknowleding to yourself how grievously and fatally you have erred. There is not one statesman amongst us who has either wisdom or virtue to set things right. It is useless to look behind for the redress of the grievances. Many people have died of starvation and it is impossible to restore them to life, but there is still a ray of hope left for those who are dying. The kindness and sympathetic treatment at the hands of Mujirud-Daulah can save them from starvation. I, therefore, beseech you to do every thing possible to ensure that in future the people will not be exploited so mercilessly. I pray that a Government circular letter be issued soon to put a stop to such irregularities on the part of Government officials in the interest of common folk whose prayers have saved your premiership from destruction. May God help you and open for you the doors of worldly and heavenly bliss and enlightenment which you are not aware of.

Your Excellency's humble servant,

Al-Ghazzali.

(14)

To His Excellency Mu'inul Mulk

In the name of Allah, the Beneficient, the Merciful.

God says:

> "As far that abode of the Hereafter We assign it unto those who seek not oppression in the earth, nor yet corruption. There sequel is for those who ward off evil". (28: 83).

Salvation is of two kinds namely (a) The rise above others through relentless struggle (b) to keep away from bad associates and from the disobedient among men. Undoubtedly the one who has ambition of conquering other countries is possessed of magnanimity and magnificence, and the one who does not restrain himself from things forbidden and from evil and sinful acts disturbs the world and pollutes it. It is futile to expect salvation without fulfilling the necessary conditions, and those who refuse to believe that salvation depends upon fulfilling the two conditions already mentioned are deceived by greed and led astray by the devil, because they do not act upon the teaching of Qur'an. It is unwise to be satisfied with wretchedness and disbelief in the next world. It will not be out of place to mention here that there are certain men who strictly observe these two conditions, yet the passions of the animal self overpower them. The reason is that they believe that God being merciful and kind would eventually forgive them, but they are not wise enough to remember that God is gracious only to those who lead good lives:--

> "The garden will be the home of the good and the hell be the abode of the evildoers". (82: 13).

On other occasions they say to themselves, "We shall start living a life of repentance from tomorrow". They know fully well that for the last several years the devil has been playing tricks with them and exploiting them with hopes for the future and preventing them repentance and doing good deeds for the present. If there lives are extended by a few years, certainly they would again resort to the same base passions and forgetfulness of the Day of Judgment. Sometimes they suppose that they would live longer than others and that good deeds could be conveniently done later on. Have they entered into an agreement with the Angel of death to this effect? Woe to them, they do not know that most of men have perished in a wretched condition, simply, because the devil misled them into false hopes. If you want to take such risks in the evening of your life, none would be more miserable and regretful than you.

> "Are the people of the townships then secure from the coming of Our wrath upon them as a night raid while they sleep? Or are the people of the townships then secure from the coming of Our wrath upon them in the day while they play? Are they then secure from Allah's scheme? None deemeth himself secure from Allah's scheme, save folk that perish". (7: 97 to 99).

May you and all of us awake from deep sleep of indifference, and may Mu'inul Mulk be warned against what one of his friends has told me these days. The things reported to me against him are the source of incalculable danger in respect of Hereafter. So far as he is concerned, I have become extremely worried. There is nothing at my disposal except a deep feeling of devotion, good wishes, verbal warnings and written advice which I have exclusively reserved for him. Though you do not feel pity towards yourself, let me look at yourself with the look of mercy.

You amuse yourself with drinking wine that blinds your eyes and heart to your duties towards your people and an understanding of the laws of human nature. I advise you to renounce drinking wine, even if it is so hard for you to severe your ties with the cruel and corrupt Government officials, for when personal sin is associated with cruelty, it is beyond human power to get them separated from each other, particularly, in one's old age drinking wine is one of the worst crimes. Nizamul Mulk renounced the major sins including drinking wine and other wicked things when the frost of age was upon his head. Till the last days of his life he resolutely maintained in full vigour the religious pledge that he would never drink wine or abandon repentance. He used to say: "If the king of Khurasan does not despise the things prohibited by Him, the Lord of the kingdoms of earth and heaven would not forgive him and no excuse would be acceptable to Him."

I sincerely hope you would despise wine and make up your mind to hate it for the rest of your days. I have said these things in the interest of friendship which has mutually developed between us.

Your Excellency's humble servant,
Al-Ghazzali.

(15)

To His Excellency Sa'adat Khan

In the name of Allah, the Beneficient, the Merciful.

God says:

> "And there is not a thing but with Us are the stores thereof. Any We send it not down save in appointed measures". (15: 21).

The treasures belonging to the kings are limited; while the treasurehouse of bounties belonging to the Owner of the Kingdoms of earth and heaven is infinite. One of these treasures is His blessings and the other His curse, and both of them lie hidden mysteriously. There are two keys to them. One is called obedience and the other sin. These keys lie in the two treasures of God to whom all mysterious things are disclosed. One of these keys is also known as Divine guidance and the other disappointment. The pearls of success and failure are contained in other mysterious treasures. One of them is widely known as contentment and the other anger, and the pearls of contentment and anger are also found in the two treasures, which are beyond the reach of the vulgar who cannot even catch the glimpses of these pearls. There are mysteries about spiritual realities which will always remain unexplored. These are the types of ecstatic state, of inspiration and illumination which is a most glorious attainment that cannot be expressed by knowledge. As for most of the learned and the enlightened, they are not pre-eminent for an authentic first hand intimate personal knowledge of God. The inner secrets of faith are purposely shrouded in mystery and carefully hidden from the learned. The mysterious gift of mystic apprehension is bestowed upon elect souls, not for their own glory but for the sake of the whole humanity; to gauge the mysteries, we must gauge them with the mystics, for the ground of mysteries and the mystics are one and the same,

God refers to them thus:

"Those for whom We have already reserved good reward." (21: 101).

They are the persons who know the secrets of these treasures. Besides, those of whom:

"Truth has dawned upon most of them" (36:7) has been said are competent enough to disclose those things. Both of these holy verses refer to a secret which is the most wonderful of all mysteries. The height of wisdom is to remain quite dumb and silent about these realities. There must be absolute stillness and distraction must cease.

One should be carefully watchful of what one utters in the respect. Fate is a secret of God, which should never be disclosed at all costs.

There is another treasure lying beyond these closely guarded treasures from which all the treasures originate. Words fail to convey what this really is. The Holy Prophet reached this stage step by step. First he said, after making the profession of faith.

"Through thy pardon my soul seek refuge with Thee". Then he said:

"With Thy will I seek shelter from Thy wrath".

Then he was visited by spiritual forces which he had never known before and he said:

"I seek shelter from Thee in Thee".

Then he was promoted to a higher rank till he said:

"I cannot praise Thee. Thou art as glorious as Thou hast praised Thyself".

The learned attain to the rank explained in:

اعـوذ بـرضائك من سخطك

They cannot reach beyond this, and the prophets alone have access to the inmost and highest secrets of being as mentioned in اعوذ بك منك . There is another world beyond all this where neither the Prophet can reach, nor the most learned. It is their steady and unremitting struggle with themselves which enables them in the end to catch a glimpse of this wonderful world, to their utter astonishment and fear. Soon they begin to be consumed in the fire of humiliation and misery, as a result of the love they bear for their Beloved and being to declare steadily, "The most praise-worthy! The most holy!" The Holy Prophet has confessed in these words:

"I cannot praise Thee. Thou art as glorious as Thou hast praised Thyself".

Abu Bakr Siddiq who was the most faithful witness of the truth used to state: "My power has failed me and the transcendent truths of the spiritual world are quite beyond my natural apprehension". Sometimes he suffered seriously due to extreme humility and powerlessness, which on other occasions, mistaking modesty for natural apprehension his joy knew no bounds. This is an account of the treasures belonging to the king of heaven and earth and these are the exhilarating sights relating to them. So far as the hoards of silver and gold in possession of the kings of this world are concerned, suffice it to say that they are the keys to hell.

"The worshippers of gold and silver will certainly perish".

A proclamation will be made on the Day of Judgement, "Open the doors of the treasures of hell, and bring those to our court whose names are mentioned in the records maintained by Our angels".

Suppose the poor Sa'adat Khan finds his name included therein what will he do? Neither the Sultan of the Seljuk Empire will support him that day, nor the Amirs and viziers will come to help him, as they would themselves stand in need of supporters.

Your Excellency's humble servant,

Al-Ghazzali.

(16)

To one of the Amirs

In the name of Allah, the Beneficient, the Merciful.

The disorders of the human organism which is the most intricate and complex structure in the world, and the exact means of putting them right are the most difficult and complex study, and being so, they yield a large scope for fallacies of observation and inference.

Many, therefore, are the false theories and many the monstrous remedies for them, so man and great errors and evils having flowed from wrong observation and reasoning, it is natural for me to be full of worries. The physicians who try to cure these diseases, as if they proceed from natural causes are ignorant persons who know nothing of medicine. The truth of the matter is that the One Who creates diseases is the One Who knows how to cure them, but the vulgar believe that medicine should be bought from chemist, according to the prescription of a physician, and then used as directed. This is the most serious error. It it, through the mercy and guidance of God Almighty that the patient selects the most suitable doctor for his treatment and again it is through Divine Revelation that the physician prescribes the best remedy, taking into account the suitable quantity and quality of the medicine which is to be used with due regard to time and interval, for if a doctor ignores these important factors, he is of no use to the patient who will ultimately abandon his treatment as useless or pernicious. The best and most reliable medicines are not obtained from the shops of chemists, because the key to them lies in the treasure of the angels who are the agents responsible for the administration of affairs of the kingdom of heaven. By Allah's command men are provided with the most useful guidance by the angels under whose control heavenly treasures are placed, as laid down in the Holy qur'an:

> "And it was not (vouchsafed) to any mortal that Allah should speak to him unless (it be) by revelation or from behind a veil or that He sendeth a messenger to reveal that He wills by His leave. Lo! He is Exalted Wise". (43: 51).

If the best cure is to be sincerely sought, it is always to be found in the prayers of the holy and it is through the agency of the angels that the afflicted persons feel the heavenly drop upon their souls:

> "And there is not a thing but with Us are the stores thereof. And We send it not down save in appointed measures". (15: 21).

You cannot avail, yourself of the devotional spirit of the pious unless you benefit them by almsgiving and kindness. Almsgiving brings relief both for the doctor and his patient and provides the patient with the most effective remedy borrowed from the treasures placed in the custody of the angels are revealed in the hadith, "Get rid of your diseases through almsgiving". What then is that about which we ought to employ our serious thoughts. This one thing that there is no god but Allah Whose goodness overflows all things and whose inner power animates the innermost hearts which hence become wider than the heaven and earth. The eternal God is found at a point within ourselves, which as the mystics hold, is equally God's central reality and ours, where spirit with spirit meets. "They will ask thee concerning the spirit. Say: The spirit is by command of my Lord". (17: 85).

These things are too difficult to understand and God has forbidden as to disclose the mysteries about the human soul. It is not wise to waste one's time on what man cannot understand. However, it is sufficient for us to know that the spirit and spiritualism are inseparable and proportionate to each other, since the time that this planet was first created, no research scholar in any age, and of any country has been able to discover this closely-guarded secret on the basis of this vast knowledge and experiments with truth. In short, care depends upon almsgiving which is linked with prayers that bring health and healing to the body and produces a rare clarity of mind and enhances moral and spiritual power, therefore, it is said that prayers keep away all sorts of suffering and troubles.

And it is mentioned in the hadith that:

"Prayers and disorder struggle with each other".

Prayers are like assembled armies that invade and wipe out all the sources of evil and mischief, prayers for rains and congregational worship in mosques explain this point, and we have seen on many occasions in response to the prayers of the pious, refreshing and life giving showers fall on the parched ground and the desert is made to blossom as the rose. A specialist in metaphysics can question my knowledge in this regard and argue that the diseases caused by fever requires cool medicines for their treatment. There is no reason why almsgiving could not be effective in such disorder. Doctors have made mistakes before. Why should not they be wrong now? They fail to realise that the human organism which is a fabric of such complicated correlations of parts and functions that the more the mechanism is known, the more the wonder grows that it ever keep itself in working order so well and for so long as it does. This is not due to one's efforts for keeping good health. It is all due to the grace of the merciful Allah. A metaphysician, being misled by faulty observation arrives at the conclusion that a variety of external influence have caused the ailment and his shortsightness is responsible for his jumping at the wrong conclusion. His eyes fail to see the depths and the summit of the human soul in which there is a principle untouched by external influences, which flows from spirit, remaining in the spirit itself, altogether spiritual in its content. In this principle is God, ever verdant, flowering in all the joy and glory of His actual self and no man can in any wise behold it. An example will explain this. Suppose an ant walking along a piece of paper beholds that a line is caused by a pen. It can see neither the heart of the writer where the idea of writing has taken place, nor the writer's hand which is the real mover of the pen. In this example human nature is a pen, the angels are the fingers holding the pen and God Almighty to Whom all the angels bow in obedience is like the hand and the possessor of it. It was the pen of God which at His command wrote down the simple Natures and in the twinkling of an eye started into being, the intelligence, souls, Elements and Natures, the Heavens and the stars. These then took up the task and obeyed the second mandate by writing down the compound bodies and straightway the mineral, vegetable and Animal Kingdoms sprang into existence. These are the scribes of God and the words they write are the compound bodies of nature. Since men is finite he cannot see the Infinite or His work. He can only see the pen, but it is not the pen that writes but the holder of it. Man does not fully understand that His Knowledge, Will and Power comprehend and pervade the whole range of natural causes and effects. He fails to observe that causes as well as effects yield and are subservient to His Will and attribute every event to the action of some natural law.

> "The hearts of the believers lie between the two fingers of the Beneficent":
>
> "So like Himself God made Adam that nothing else in earth or heaven resembles God so closely as does the man".
>
> "And he who knoweth his own self, knoweth God."

The mind of the writer, his hand and fingers are above the pen and his body lies below, He alone is the wisest who rise stage by stage from the lowest level to the highest spiritual stage.

"Surely We created man of the best structure. Then We reduced him to the lowest of the low." (95: 4, 5). It is a pity that some people believe in the miraculous cures by a doctor.

A policy of total reliance on medical aid would be disastrous. When we are ill, the best course left upon to us is that we should surrender ourselves entirely, taking refuge with God, as men in sore affliction, who have no other resources or supporters left. If one is pious and learned, his prayer can easily reach the Malakute world of self which is the highest of the high. This height is not to be reached with an astronomic ladder to stars or with the wings of an angel. Perception or intelligence can never lead to his conviction or reveal this glorious mystery, that is the province of the Divine

Light alone. Wealth and dignity have strayed away many from the right path, they are the gods people worship. Renunciation is the practice of those who know God and the characteristic mark of the wise, if then you see that one has expelled the love of this from his heart you may be sure that he will arrive at his destination. The guide that shall conduct him on his path assumes the form of good words.

> "Good deeds would elevate him to the contemplation of spiritual things through the medium of his most impressionable feelings".

One cannot attain to the good of life by distributing breads and meat among those who do not pray, for it would only add to the greed of the needy and their desires. Such almsgiving should be exclusively confined in respect of holy and God-fearing. Now there is no mercy better than to devote one's self to the perfection and improvement of others both by precept and example. It is essential that almsgiving should be strictly and confidentially confined to those "Faqirs" who are pure in spirit and in their lives, and who, in spite of their best efforts are too poor to support their families. If they are benefited both temporally and spiritually, they would surely pray for the well being of their benefactors and thus the services of a specialist who knows how to treat the physical and spiritual diseases by heavenly guidance would be readily available. There is no approach from unaided sense to the cure of the mind or the body. It is unwise to depend upon the treatment by those who do not know what medicine is. Every doctor fancies that he alone possesses the knowledge of medicine but this is an attribute of the mind and unless one is possessed of this knowledge, one cannot say for certain whether he or is not an expert physician.

Yours sincerely,
Al-Ghazzali.

(17)

To The Administrative Heads of all Government Departments

In the name of Allah, the Beneficient, the Merciful.

God says:

> "And whose doeth good an atom's weight will see it then, And whoso doeth ill an atom's will see it then." (95: 7, 8).

Man's conduct, his speech, silence and generosity or avarice are either a glorious treasure which he cannot part with, or these are the seeds of wretchedness which he sows in all direction. Though he is indifferent to what he does, yet the guardian angels record every good or ill that he does. God is always near to those who seek Him, while those only are far removed from Him who do not remember Him, and who by their actions fail to acknowledge that He is Omnipresent and Omniscient, knowing and seeing all they do. The moment man dies, a register of his deeds from the early period of his life to the end of his days is shown to him:--

> "On the day every soul will find itself confronted with all that it hath done of good and all that it hath done of evil, (every soul) will long that there might be a mighty space of distance between it and that (evil)". (3: 30).

Then good having an atom's weight would be placed in one scale and ill having the same quantity would be placed in another, and man would be subjected to the verdict of a balance (Mizan) and he would be awfully worried and anxious to know which of the scales rises and falls:--

> "Then, as for him, whose scales are heavy (with good) he will live a pleasant life. But as for him, whose scales are light, Hell will be nursing mother to him. And what should

make thee know what that is? It is a blazing Fire". (101: 6 to 11).

On that day the scales of the rich would be light, for they spent their money to satisfy their animal passions and the scale of the humble would be heavy, because they used their money in carrying out the commandments of God. Those who have much are often greedy, those who have little always share. Those who spend their whole wealth in almsgiving attain to perfect salvation, no doubt to escape the danger involved in worldly possession. Abu Bark Siddiq disposed of his estate and large property and placed the proceeds at the feet of the Holy Prophet (peace and blessings of Allah be upon him). When asked as to what he had left for his dependents. Abu Bakr Siddiq (may Allah be pleased with him) replied: "I am sure God and His Messenger can confer on me a substantial benefit sufficient to relieve me from anxiety concerning the means of the subsistence of my family". This happened when the Prophet once declared, "The rich have perished and he alone has survived who has scattered his wealth in all directions, helping the poor and carrying out the commandments of God". Since a man is miserly by nature and does not want to spend his money except in his own personal interest, therefore, it is incumbent upon him to spend his money only upon those who are really in need of his financial help, so that God may reward him with manifold increase on the Day of Judgment, when the exchange value for £1.00 (given to the needy) would be equal to more than £1000.00. The money gifted by a rich man must be honestly earned and distributed among the pious and the learned, who have no source of income to fall upon in hard times. God says:

"O ye, who believe! Render not vain your almsgiving by laying obligation and injury". (2: 264).

Yours sincerely,

Al-Ghazzali.

(18)

To Qazis of Maghrib-i-Aqsa

In the name of Allah, the Beneficient, the Merciful.

"Praise be to Allah, Lord of the worlds. Salvation is confined to the believers, and His wrath would strike down those who are cruel, and I testify that our master Muhammad (peace be upon him and his descendants) is the head and chief of His Messengers". It is mainly due to the efforts of Imam Marwan a distinguished Judge that a mere acquaintance between myself and honorable Sardar Mu'tamadul Mulk Amin-ud-Daula has ripened into a deep friendship which is dearer to me than if he were one of my nearest relatives for he is the greatest mystic in the mystical movement of today and one of the greatest mystics of the whole of Islamic history. I do not remember whether or when I have sent him a written reminder of my affection, but in the moments of leisure, it has struck me that there has been a disproportionate silence between us. It is essential, therefore, that we should write to each other more frequently. To promote the friendship which already exists between us, I would like to employ a rich counsel which I offer you as a gift from the learned. I want to let you know that if you want to know the right and avoid ignorance you should cultivate a disposition which gladly accepts association with the wise. The Prophet (peace and blessings of Allah be upon him) was asked: "Who is the best of men". He said: "The one who is the most pious among them". He was further asked, "Who is the wisest?" He replied: "The one who remembers death and is always prepared for it". It is laid down in a hadith, "He is alone wise who is a master of his self and ignorant is the one who is a slave to his desires". Surely he is the most wretched fellow who is not revivified and illumined and it is impossible for him to attain to intelligence at all. The intelligence is a light in the heart, distinguishing between truth and vanity. The intelligent person casts away the love of worldly objects and lives in submission and resignation to His will, while on the other hand it does not appeal to the ignorant whether his abode would be in the Paradise or Hell. God has clarified the situation in the plainest of words:

> "Those who do good works would enter Paradise, and the evil-doers would be cast into Hell".
>
> (82: 12).

In another place God says:

> "The, as for him, who rebelled and chose the life of the world, Lo! Hell will be his home. But as for him who feared to stand before his Lord and restrained his soul from lust, Lo! the garden will be his home". (79: 37 to 41).

Again God says:

> "Whoso desireth the life of the world and its pomp, we shall repay them their deeds therein, and therein they will not be wronged. Those are they for whom is naught in the Hereafter save the Fire (all) that they contrive here is gain and (all) that they are wont to do is fruitless". (11: 15, 16).

The universe is the mirror of the universe, if you then would know God, and the heart of man is the mirror of the universe, if you then would know God, you must look into your own heart. The guide that shall conduct you on your path is there "a still small voice", that ever bids you "eschew the evil and choose the good". It is the heart that promises freedom from hasty judgment and friendship towards men and obedience to God. It will certainly lead you to the goal of eternal bliss. When you turn to the very innermost deepest consciousness of your real self you have a perception of indwelling of God within you realizing that to turn inward to the light within you is to live in the presence of God or your divine self, you soon discover the unreality of the objects to which you have hitherto been turning and which have engrossed you without, and when yourself moves the heart in search of any object of desire and any enjoyment and the heart responds to this demand for the object and thus without any command from God and His permission. The result is forgetfulness of God and sin. God seizes them (the mind, and the heart) with ignominy and calamities and subjection to people and injury and anxiety and pain and disease. You should open your eyes and look into the future and find out what good deeds you have done for tomorrow. Remember none is more sympathetically inclined towards you than your own heart. Think deeply for a minute or two and decide what it is that you run after. Perhaps you are dissatisfied with that which is assigned to you out of the universe and you want to found a city? If so, consider:

"And how many cities We have destroyed". (7: 3).

If you want to dig up wells or canals, think how many of them have fallen into ruins with time. If you intend to build a grand house, remember how fast the magnificent buildings, already erected have disappeared and if you want to lay out a beautiful garden read:

> "How many were the gardens and the watersprings that they left behind. And the corn lands and the good sites and pleasant things wherein they took delight! Even so (it was) and We made it an inheritance for other folk: And the heaven and the earth wept not for them, nor were they reprieved".
>
> (44: 25 to 29).

And read the following verses of the Holy Qur'an:

> "Hast then thou seen, if We contend themselves (long) years, And then came that which they were promised (How) that where with they were contented naught availeth them?" (26: 205).

God forbid, if you want to serve the king, you should read this hadith; On the Day of Resurrection the kings and the viziers would rise like ants from earth and the common folk would tread them roughly under their feet. If you are not satisfied with this read what God said in connection with:

"There is an oppressor for every proud man".

The Prophet has said:

"Let people mourn for him (in his lifetime) who indulges in pride and cherishes a desire to become a chief among men".

He has also said:

"Two wolves cannot harm a herd of sheep so much, as do the wealth and ambition cause havoc among the Muslim section of mankind".

If this is not sufficient to satisfy you, refer to a saying of Jesus Christ (peace be upon him):

"O my friends wealth is the source of worldly happiness and the cause of endless suffering in the other world. By God. I say that rich would not enter the heavenly kingdom".

The Prophet has said:

"On the Day of Resurrection the rich will rise in groups. The first group would be constituted of those who earned money legally and spent it lawfully. God would say to His angels, "Ask them if they spent their wealth on forbidden objects contrary to my commandments, or whether they disturbed the order in which they ought to have worshipped Me, by committing mistakes in the performance of ablution and in kneeling before Me properly. It is also possible that they did not give due attention to charity and pilgrimage and "Zakat" which are to be performed with appropriate attention to deatil and the utmost solemnity and decorum. Addressing the angel they would explain, "We amassed wealth through honest means, and performing the obligatory duties, we spend it in the name of Allah and did not misappropriate a single penny". Then they would be asked: "Did you show mercy to those of mankind who were poor and did you give your neighbours their due?"

Meanwhile a crowd of men would appear from the opposite direction prostrating and crying: "Our Lord! They were the richest men among us and you had forced us to stand in need of their financial help, and yet they did not care to help us". Accordingly, they would be chained, dragged and thrown into Hell". This will be the fate of those who earn money legally and spend it on the welfare of His servants. God alone knows what will happen to those whose lifetime runs out, while they hoard gold for their personal benefit. There are the people who would be punished and incur the wrath of God. Being lost in the desires of the flesh, they are never shaken awake:

> "Rivalry in the worldly increase distracteth you until ye come to the graves. Nay, but ye will come to know!" (102: 1 to 3).

There are the false hopes and base desires which have subdued human hearts trapped by the devils. If a disease takes toot in one's heart, it can only be treated by one who is an enemy towards his self. Intellectual cure is more important than physical treatment. They alone are immune from spiritual ailments who are possessed of pure hearts. There are two kinds of medicines suggested for the treatment of heart troubles. The first consists in remembering death and meditating upon it always, taking into account the dreadful end of the fallen kings and the worshippers of wealth--how they amassed immense riches, built magnificent palaces and wasted their lives in pride and hypocrisy, till death walked silently towards them, and turning their palaces into graveyards obliterated all traces of their pomp and grandeur.

> "Is it not a guidance for them (to know) how many a generation we destroyed before them, amid whose dwellings they walk? Lo! therein verily are signs for men of thought". (20: 128).

Their palaces and houses which now lie in the ruins, tell their story, and again there are others who have disappeared even from fables. The second medicine prescribed for healing the human heart is to meditate deeply upon the contents of the Holy Qur'an which contains the best cure and divine blessings. On his death-bed the Prophet advised us to keep in touch with two advisers. He said:

"I have left two advisers among you, who sometimes speak to you, while on other occasions they prefer silence. One of them is the Qur'an and the other the Laws of His Messenger".

"You will not stray as long as you hold the fast". Though the people look alive, yet in reality they are dead, for they have lost all interest in the Book of God. They read the Qur'an with their tongues, no doubt, but actually they are dumb. They also hear it being read out of them, but in actual practice they are dead. They see it wrapped up in an expensive silk-cloth, and placed in an almirah, yet they are blind to its meanings and mysteries. They explain the meaning of the Book of God in their commentaries, yet they themselves are quite ignorant as they do not follow the teachings of the Holy Qur'an. They know that Satan is their enemy, but they do not deal with him as such. I warn you against falling into deception by joining the company of such men as have gone astray from the right path and do not perform the obligatory duties. Low desires and passions of the baser self overpower them and they are cut off from God's help. So, if death overtakes them before repentance, they shall be among the perished ones. There is a verse in the Holy Qur'an which provides the enlightened with a true light and guidance:--

> "O ye who believe! Let not your wealth nor your children distract you from remembrance of Allah. Those who do so, they are the losers". (63: 4).

Beware lest you indulge in the accumulation of wealth for this kind of happiness will create inner discords which will interfere with the absorption of consciousness in spiritual things, and force you to forget the Day of Resurrection. The Holy Prophet has said: Such terrible doom would befall those who look at the wealth of others with eyes full of greed. It is beyond human power to imagine what endless suffering lies in store for those who hoard wealth and waste their lives in open rebellion against God's commandments. So far as the great Qadi Imam Marwan is concerned, I pray my God save and preserve him for he is an eminent Sufi, a perfect devout and highly pious. He is possessed of both extraordinary intellectual power and fear of God, and these virtues will develop into a definite and permanent form only when his father helps him and contributes towards a better understanding of his son, who being one of the most prominent philosophers and mystics of 'Iran, is an organ for bringing peace and prosperity for his father both here and hereafter. With uplifted hands and eyes he should pray for his son, who being a spiritual seer, call for a new epoch of faith and life and power and from whose great soul our Islamic faith can and will be reborn. He is not a "rebel or a wilful heretic". He is a spiritual seer and has brought out of his store-house things both new and old. He is essentially loyal to Islam, but he speaks in a new tongue and it sounds strange to the guardians of the old heritage. The goal of life can only be attained when we are constant and firm in love and accept with delight and without any grudge all troubles and pains received from the friend, contrary to the practice of the evil-doers who sell the next world for the sake of money. You cannot expect salvation, unless you severe all ties with the Sultans and Amirs. One of the traditions says that the learned are the tustees of Allah, so long as they have nothing to do with the worldly objects, you should bear in mind that they are far away from religion and that you renounce their worldly ambitions. Allah has opened to you the knowledge of these things which are not difficult to achieve. It is, therefore, your sacred duty to be or amiable terms with your son, so that you may be benefited by his prayers. Remember, the humble prayers which escape from the hearts of one's soul are the key to the contemplative life and the source of a great relief in respect of the parents, both in this world and in the next.

You should act upon your son's advice, so far as it is concerned with the renunciation of the basic desires and the alluring temptations of the self, because though a son is like a branch, yet through good deeds he can be likened to full fledged tree. That is what Hadrat Ibrahim (peace be upon him) said:

> "O my father Lo! There hath come unto me of knowledge that which cause not unto thee. So follow me and I will lead thee on a right path".
>
> (19: 43).

You should treat your son with kindness. He should be as dear to you as your own soul. When the people of this world would be raised in the life hereafter, they would earnestly desire that someone should recommend them to Allah.

God says:

"He has no friend here today". (69: 35).

I pray God Almighty may make this world appear a contemptible thing in your eyes, as it is to Him and delight you with the realm of the spiritual and Real which could be desired. May we severe all the bonds of convention and follow God's will and the track which leads to eternal life in Paradise.

Yours sincerely,

Al-Ghazzali.

(19)

To Khwaja Imam 'Abbasi

In the name of Allah, the Beneficient, the Merciful.

Someone asked the Prophet: "Inform me, in the matter of Islam, so that I may have no occasion to ask others about it". He replied: "Say, I believe in God, after which firmly obey the commands and abandon the things forbidden".

To believe in God means that God and the spiritual world are ever present realities in the routine of our daily life. Islam teaches us that in order to devote exclusive attention to fulfilling our duties to God and to our fellow beings, we must abandon all vain and useless activities which distract us from this end. When we are enlightened with the true light, we renounce all desires and commit and commend ourselves and all things to Allah. Then we are in a state of freedom, because we have lost the fear of pain or hell and the hope of reward or heaven, and are living in pure submission to Allah. We reduce our cognitive faculties to zero, to absolute inaction and in this sacred silence contemplate things divine, by union not in ourselves, but by going out of ourselves entirely and becoming wholly of God. The universe has flowed out from Him. It is a divine emanation and there is also a cosmic process of "return" back to the eternal one. The only possible approach, therefore, is the ways of negation. The stage of obeying God's commandments comes next.

The abandonment of the things forbidden consists in three things--the heart should be purified of all the inner impurities--we should improve our conduct so that other men may be improved--and thankfulness for the blessings of comfort in the limbs and the organs of the body is to use them in carrying out the commandments of God and in restraining ourselves from things forbidden and from evil and sinful acts. One should always weigh his words and deeds. Wisdom means the intelligent weighing of both sides of a situation and the finding out of the right middle course between two extremes. It is, therefore, very important that we should subject ourselves to the verdict of a balance and discover whether our scale shall rise or fall. When man's self comes across the objects of pleasure, it naturally insists that they should be obtained for the time being and that they would be abandoned next time. The best course left open to us in this condition is that we should ask our "self" to abstain this time from gaining the objects and that it would be more advisable to obtain them next time. We should take our "self" nor more seriously than it takes us. We have the right to restore to a sort of personal reprisal. In this way we return to the right quarter jest for jest; we play the trick that has been played on us. If we cannot practise this continuously, at least we can make ourselves as familiar with it as possible. It is the recollection of God, the thought of God which in all places and circumstances make us see Him present. Let us commune respectfully and lovingly with Him and full ourselves with the desire and affection of Him. Never lose sight of the idea of God neither in prosperity nor in adversity, nor on any occasion, whatsoever it may be. Let your mundane activities of your life may not absorb you to such an extent that you may ignore the Lord. Bear this fact always in your mind that God sees you, that you are under His eyes. If a thousand time an hour you forget Him, try to remember Him for two thousand time an hour. If beneath the weight of over-powering misery or in the intoxication of unwanted prosperity, you should waver for a moment in your belief in God, you should atone for your error at once, by a long and earnest course of penitence and prayer. We usually make the ideals of life those material things which do not give us peace and happiness. If we remember God and worship Him, peace and happiness should come of themselves as necessary and as the mere outcome or natural result of a far higher life permeated with spirituality through and through. This life is the real seeking of the kingdom of God and the desire for His supremacy in our hearts. If we are able to live such a life, we would deserve salvation, peace of mind and divine grace both here and Hereafter.

Yours sincerely,
Al-Ghazzali.

(20)

To Abul Hassan Mas'ud bin Muhammad bin Ghanam

In the name of Allah, the Beneficient, the Merciful.

I have received your letter full of knowledge and the mystics experience through which it is vitally incorporated into your personality. It was so long since I had heard from you that I felt a degree of uneasiness at your silence and I thought so much of your letter that to abandon the thought was a considerable disappointment. The receipt of your letter has gratified me and warmed my heart. It happened that I was thinking about you at the moment when your letter came, but this is not so extraordinary coincidence as it might seem, for you have been in my thoughts every day during my extensive travels. I think that the one thing which has impressed me most is learning the fact that you have acquired such sterling qualities of character like humility, modesty, truthfulness and wisdom and practical ability of a very high order is joined with these virtues. I am glad to know that you have devoted your whole life to the pursuit of spiritual knowledge, for which you are putting your best efforts like a sane and vigorous person, who travels on the path of righteousness, perform good deeds through his learning and gathers the fruit of his labours before death and shall not regret the passing away of his days. You should always bear in mind that the beginning of the performance of good deeds involves a steady obedience to the will of Allah, Who keeps your mind at ease and your thoughts in even course at the end. I am deeply interested to find that you are well-versed in literature and the religious laws. Don't be satisfied with what you have already gained, for it would be unwise to think that being a finite human being, you have comprehended the whole range of knowledge which is infinite.

> "The knowledge the wisest men have shared of Thy great power and Thee, is less when with Thyself compared, than one drop in a sea".

Not till your renounce the worldly desires and exchange unimportant business for positive knowledge and humility for honour, you shall not be fit to be called enlightened. Intellect working by itself is incapable of realizing the eternal value of man. This value lies in the spiritual serenity which you must always try to realize and attain. Your action righteously is your return to the real nature of man. for when you have finished your upward progress and reached this, you are in Paradise and in the presence of your Lord. The best knowledge is the science of religion which is most beneficial to mankind, and your object should, therefore, be to learn it and preach it among your fellow men so that the human soul may be strengthened and purified by renunciation and contemplation, until it reflects the true light, which is the spirit of the Humanity. The love and regard for the oppressed enable one to receive from God Almighty the reward of many years' prayers. One fourth of worship consists in the administration of justice, i.e. giving every man his due. Many people entrapped into ambition and worldly gain are divided and have degenerated to such an extent that many of their acts and deeds are not only repulsive and repugnant to Islam, but are indeed flagrant violations of its basic tenets. Something must be done before the wrath of God seizes them. Though the knowledge of the laws relating to the administration of justice among men is indispensable, yet it is quite insignificant when compared with the knowledge of Divinity, which lights our way to heaven and revives our spirit by its rich fragrance. True knowledge leads us to a stage where we can remove the cobwebs of alien philosophers from the real Islamic thought and separate truth from falsehood, in order to save the Muslims from doubts and deviation. The duty of acquiring true knowledge can be easily performed by one who is a specialist in the interpretation of spiritual realities. If he commits an error in the interpretation in spite of his utmost endeavour, he is rewarded for his sincerity and if he does not commit any mistake in the process, he is rewarded two-fold. The knowledge which enables the possessor to distinguish right from wrong is not so precious as the knowledge which provides man with eternal salvation. The spiritual remedies are only known to the spiritual healers who observe that causes as well as effects are subservient to His will. We find sufficient evidence to convince us that proper reform in mental attitude would relieve many a sufferer of ills that the ordinary physicians cannot touch and the faithful adherence to a true philosopher of life will not keep many a man well, but would also enable him to finish his upward progress and reach Paradise. In just the degree that we come into a conscious realization of our oneness with the Infinite life and open ourselves to this divine inflow, do we actualize in ourselves the qualities and powers of the Infinite life, do we make ourselves channels through which the Infinite intelligence and power can work? This sort of life is almost unrecognizeable unless we live it into ourselves actually, but what can we say to those who do not understand? This, at least, we can say that it is a life whose experiences are proved real to their possessor, because they remain with him when brought closest into contact with the objective realities of the life. "The bird which does not know what pure sweet water is, frequently dips its beak into saltish water".

I have faith in the development of your philosophical thought and rely on your great mystical knowledge which is a genuine key for un-locking the world's treasure-house to you who can use it practically. That is why, as a well-wisher, I have contributed these few lines towards your welfare; in my own human way.

Yours sincerely,

Al-Ghazzali.

(21)

To all the Prominent Theologians

In the name of Allah, the Beneficient, the Merciful.

The Holy Prophet (peace be upon him) has said: "This world is utterly vile and wicked. It has fallen into a deep abasement. Every thing it contains is cursed, save those things which are exclusively meant for God". The persons who lead the life of conventionality, artificiality and personal ambition and indulge in the accumulation of wealth, sow only the seeds of mischief and wretchedness, resulting in the devastation of the face of earth. This world is the means and the next the end. The wise man is he who collects the goods here for his journey to the Hereafter. The Prophet has hinted to the same effect in the Hadith.

> "Honestly earned money is a source of great strerigth for an honest man".

The bes of virtues is the love of regard for the learned and pious and the best of money is almsgiving to them. There is no better way of salvation than by bringing relief to the hearts of pious servants of Allah.

Yours sincerely,

Al-Ghazzali.

(22)

To Khwaja 'Abbas Khwarzam

In the name of Allah, the Beneficient, the Merciful.

Religious brotherhood and relationship in knowledge are deeply-rooted and unite two men more closely than all sorts of other relations. Apparently you are not known to me, but by spiritual contemplation I have arrived at the conclusion that you are one of those persons whom I hold most dear.

Souls before being housed in bodies were like assembled armies. One should look upon the hearts rather than upon the bodies. It is a source of great strength and pleasure to me to learn that you having come at the end of all this development of philosophical thought and mystical experience hold the unique position of being a heir to an immense intellectual and spiritual wealth. I thank God who has blessed you with religious knowledge, mystical vision and faithful adherence to the theory and practice of the companions of the Holy Prophet (peace be upon him). These have endowed you with rare virtues. I feel sure that the plan of salvation will flash upon you like a storm of light leading you to man's real goal of life, and then you will model yourself upon the companions of the Prophet, who are the models of the saintly life and the type of glorified humanity. If you inwork ceaselessly and with single minded devotion to propagate the Islamic teachings and the mystic ideas, the entire population of our country will be benefited. Inspired by your teachings they would trust in Him alone and acquiesce entire in His will.

> "And who is better in speech than him who prayeth unto his Lord and doeth right, and sayeth: Lo! I am of those who surrender (unto Him)." (41: 32)

Yours sincerely,

Al-Ghazzali.

(23)

To Ibn-ul-'Amil

In the name of Allah, the Beneficient, the Merciful.

Thank you very much for your letter containing many things about the spiritual world and God's knowledge and your sincere faith in Him.

I pray God that He may enable you to dig still deeper for the hidden pearls of your heart so that you may become sensitive to spiritual suggestions and have a quick insight into religious questions. The knowledge which provides us with things other than the fulfillment of the commandments of God and His Messenger is harmful to its possessor. Our Holy Prophet has said:

> "Whosoever is granted the maximum of knowledge, but is deprived of proper guidance stands poles apart from God."

The guiding knowledge leads you from the creatures to the Creator, from this world to the next, from pride to humility, from greed to piety, from hypocrisy to sincerity, from doubt to truth, from the slavery of those who live a life of luxury to the doctrines of the mystics. Many people think that he who is busy acquiring the religious knowledge also walks along the true path. Actually this is not so, which is a pity indeed. It is recorded in *Sahihain* "that our Holy Prophet once said:

> "The wrath of God would descend upon those who seek knowledge of God with a view of gaining some worldly ends thereby".

The trouble with the learned is that they do not realise that to hoard knowledge is more dangerous than accumulation of wealth, for wealth is intended for use in this world and is exclusively meant for man's well-being on this planet, but religious knowledge is devoted purely to religion and the heart of religion is always to be found in close contact with God in the fathomless depths of the inner life. If it is exploited to serve our personal ends here, it contributes to the gravest of the sins. Some of the sages have observed, "The hardest people in the world to argue with are those who seek religion through such illicit means as are meant for seeking themselves or their own things".

As a matter of fact, this world is a means and the next an end. Woe unto him who sells religion for worldly gains. This world is an agent and a servant and the next is the master and the ruler. They are obstinate fools who suppose that the master is a servant and vice versa. You cannot alter the Divine principles, nor rebel against the established doctrines by finding faults with His will. Natural laws do not change, though to a certain degree they appear to assume changed form in this world which is like a fast-fading shadow, because matter, while admitting reflection which it cannot resist, takes the faise appearance of motion. The world of matter and all in it is but a dream, compared to the awakening which will come to man on his deathbed. The moment he closes his eyes, the next world and the meaning of the mysterious realities are unveiled to him. Every quality assumes a bodily shape and every man becomes an animal according to the ruling passion of his earthly life. This idea is expressed in the words of the Hadith. My people will in the eternal life, rise up in groups--that is, some as apes, some as tigers and some as hogs etc. At that time the men who earned their worldly livelihood at the cost of their religious knowledge would fall into such a deep abasement that it would seem to them reasonable that all creatures in heaven and earth should rise up against them. A Divine voice will cry:

> "Now We have removed from thee thy covering and piercing is the sight this day". (50: 22)

This situation is further explained in the following words of the Holy Qur'an:

> "Couldst thou but see when the guilty hang their heads before their Lord (and say) Our Lord! We have now seen

> and heard, so send us back; we will do right, now we are sure" (32: 12).

Again a Divine voice will reply:

> "Did not We grant you a life long enough for him who reflected to reflect therein? And the warner came unto you. Now taste (the flavour of your deeds), for evil doers have no helpers". (35: 37).

The Holy Prophet has warned,

> "The thing to be most afraid of and which I am afraid of in respect of my followers is the evil learned man".

The evil learned men will have to endure endless suffering and sorrow. The learned men can be grouped under the three heads:

(1) Those who are ignorant and profane. They are possessed of a kind of learning which is not knowledge, and they neither care for, nor desire the eternal truth which is known by experience. They are described in these words of the Qur'an:

> "They are those who are indifferent to the realities of eternal life. Verily they would be the losers on the Day of Judgement". (16: 108, 109).

(2) Those whose immediate feelings have no content, and who sit holding their heads in their hands and deeply meditating upon their grief, for not having done good deeds.

(3) Those who guard the way of the ancient Muslims and their illustrious men, i.e. the companions of the Prophet as the true path of the ultimate goal--the attainment of nearness to God and final peace in the beautiful vision. When the final nearness is attained, their souls become absorbed in the Divinity. Blessed are the eyes that have seen them or those who have seen them. You do not know how fervently I wish I could see them with my own eyes. The following passage in the Qur'an refers to these three groups:

> "But of them are some who wrong themselves, and of them are some who outstrip (others) through good deeds by Allah's leave." (35: 32).

I pray God to enlist us among the most sincere of His servants, and save us from the fraud of those who indulge in worldly pleasures.

Yours sincerely,

Al-Ghazzali.

(24)

To whomsoever it may concern

In the name of Allah, the Beneficient, the Merciful.

God has reserved His bounties for those who are pious and turn away from worldly gains and vanities and avoid forbidden things. There are only a few men out of thousands, who seek knowledge in the truest sense of the term and renounce pleasure, wealth and power which are the general objects of human ambition. And of the learned those are still fewer who know those things which are based upon the overflow of gifts, not upon constrained research or wearisome struggle for acquisition, and the fewest of the men possessed of knowledge are those who make God and the spiritual world ever present realities in the routine of daily life and whose knowledge reveals to them that all interfering distractions must be removed entirely so that the heart may become purged of all that is not God. They are the ones who have the knowledge of religion and who act thereon themselves instructing others and believing that attention given in theory and practice has its proper value and proportion. They are unmistakably the most prominent and exalted religious personalities.

> "And when they become steadfast and believe firmly in Our revelations, We appoint from among them leaders who guide by Our command."
>
> (32: 24)

They are not to be included among those of whom it has been said:

> "Recite unto them the tale of him to whom We gave Our revelation but he sloughed them off, so Satan overtook him and he become of those who lead astray". (7: 174).

There are very few persons who have the aptitude for the acquisition of true knowledge and are endowed with piety.

Usually they are overtaken by the devils and the stages of their upward progress are blocked by the mischievous activities of the latter. Near relatives, friends, money and property are felt as interfering distractions in addition to rift and enmity which have ruined many a family. If they prevent a scholar from going ahead with his prospect of studies, they can be safely compared to the devils, whose sole aim is to disturb a scholar in his studies. I believe he has the making of a true scholar in him and is fit enough to be adored with the best of knowledge and enlightenment. It ought to be possible for you to provide him with the necessary facilities, to enable him to attain to the height of knowledge and perfection, for which act of kindness you will be liberally rewarded both here and Hereafter. But, if every moment you insist that he should return home without completing his course, you will definitely spoil the whole scheme of his studies, and instead of being a patron to him, you would harm him incalculably. If you do not refrain from this, you will be regarded among those who place obstacles in the way of students and prevent them form the acquisition of knowledge. Our Holy Prophet has said:

"Don't help the devils against your brothers".

A student has told me quite innocently that going home for a few days only would not interfere with his studies. Through bitter experience I have learnt that if the link is broken, once, it is impossible to resume studies, for the home or the native village is such a store-house of mental worries, and discouragements that the pursuits of studies has to be dispensed with. I have said these things as one of your well wisher. Every man has been assigned a special duty, and it is easy for one to perform the duty for which he has been created and the blessed is the man who has been created to do good deeds and help others in this connection.

"To every Science its own people; And each man finds easy that for which he has been created apt".

Yours sincerely,

Al-Ghazzali.

(25)

To Qadi Imam Sa'eed 'Imadud-din Muhammad-Al-Wazzan

In tne name of the Allah, the Beneficient, the Merciful.

I am very glad to hear the news that some of the administrators of the affairs of your country are sparing no pains to ensure the eternal security and implement wide ranging reforms to alleviate the sufferings of the common man. All the believers are like one self united on the basis of piety and relationship in knowledge, acquaintance with one another and co-operation among themselves. Among many treasures, the pearl of the greatest price is the knowledge we have of the ancient Muslims who recognized God as the causer of all causes and relied fully upon Him, rather than upon their own energy and efforts or upon the things of this world. Those indeed are the wisest of men who act in accordance with what the ancient Muslims preached or did. They alone are to be admired and congratulated who collect goods that shall accompany them on the last journey. There are people whose philosophy is that one must avoid contemplating the thought of the next world and just enjoy as best as one can, the pleasures of life that it has to offer at the moment. They are completely devoid of spiritual capacity and composed entirely of material stuff. If they are not shaken awake some day, they will certainly bring evil on themselves through their own folly and they will be seized by God's wrath sooner or later. Since unnecessary correspondence is a kind of formality and a mere waste of time which I do not like, I resort to it only when in view of my urgent requirements I cannot possibly avoid it. God says:

> "There is no good in much of their secret conferences, save (in) him who enjoineth almsgiving, kindness and peace

> making among the people. Whoso doeth that seeking the good pleasure of Allah, We shall bestow on him a vast reward".
>
> (4:113)

Thus it would appear that correspondence too is a sort of a convention and a secret conference held for the purpose of seeking advice from others. I have a special favour to ask abruptly. That is why this letter is being written. I have a friend, the dearest one I have ever had. I cannot tell you how much I like him or what varied and extraordinary talents he possesses. His readiness for any idea in mysticism is the despair of other sufis and this fact has impressed me with his gifts. Time is against him, but he toils relentlessly to assert his individuality. He wants to seek an interview with you, for which purpose he has set on a journey to your place. He would be extremely grateful if you would receive him with regards and help him, in so far as it lies with you, for which kindness God will favour you with His mercy and bounties.

Yours sincerely,

Al-Ghazzali.

(26)

To all those who want to live a peaceful and pious life

In the name of Allah, the Beneficient, the Merciful.

One has to cross many difficult stages and surmount apparently insurmountable difficulties before one attains to spiritual height by completing upon his onward march. The most important of these stages could be summed up in two words: Social affair and gnosis. Social affair is an introduction to gnosis and begins with eating a mouthful of simple victuals earned by hard labour and ends in the sincerity of our actions and deeds. When this stage is reached, the chapter on gnosis written by the pen of God in His own book flashes before our sight and we find that the chapter is entitled:

"There is no god but Allah".

The Prophet has said:

> "The first words which God wrote in His first Book were:
> "There is no god but I, My Kindness exceeds My Wrath."

The chapter on social affair also bears the same words, but since it covers only one aspect of faith, it cannot reflect the virtues contained in gnosis. It is unwise to give a detailed account of gnosis, for the more one seeks words to express it (*ma'rifat*), the more one feels the impossibility of describing the thing by any of our usual images. A hint in this connection may be of some use to those who are interested. Gnosis or *ma'rifat* is a knowledge given in ecstasy peculiar to saints who behold God with their hearts. This knowledge differs altogether from intellectual and traditional knowledge (*'ilm*) on the other hand the more one seeks to discuss social affair in detail, the more one feels it is easily understood by the listeners, and as such it is beneficial to them. I have already said that social affair (*mu'amilah*) starts with eating a mouthful of well-earned victuals. There are four kinds of piety and devotion meant for those who eat well-earned food.

One in which the observance of justice is essential. According to the verdict of the religious *'ulema'*, pious people are required to avoid forbidden things--

Another in which good persons are not misled by doubts, even though these doubts are not declared illicit by the *Shari'at.* The Holy Prophet said to some of his companions:

> "In spite of the verdict of the *muftis* in your favour, always turn to your own conscience for a legal decision."

In other place he said:

> "Leave altogether that which is doubtful and choose that which you do not suspect."

This kind of piety is not obligatory. It is an optional virtue and contributes to man's moral progress.

The third kind signifies the devotional spirit of the worshipper. The Prophet has said:

> "Man cannot become pious, unless he avoids even the legitimate and harmless objects fearing lest they should involve him in trouble".

This is the reason why Hadrat Abu Bakr Siddiq used to place stones on his mouth to hold his tongue, so as not to run the risky by speaking something which may not be very desirable or of falling into some sin of which he might not be aware. It so happened that once Hadrat 'Umar bin Khattab smelt a diffusing musk lying in the government treasury. As he touched it, the odour spread on one of his fingers. He used to wash his finger continually and rub it against the earth so that the fragrance may be removed completely. Though there was no harm in it, yet he feared that if he indulged in strong smelling substances he might commit the sin of excessive smelling.

The fourth kind relates to the piety of the true believers who abstain from the world and its wickedness, and whose minds' eye perceive the vision of the beauty of the presence which at one glance fills their minds to the exclusion of all other objects. If they eat, they shall eat for Allah, if they drink, they drink for Allah, if they speak, they shall speak for Allah, if they live, they shall live for Allah--all their affairs are from Allah, in Allah and by Allah. God said:

> "My servant draws nigh unto Me by means of voluntary righteous acts, and I love him; and when I love him, I am his ear, so that he hears by Me, and his eye, so that he sees by Me and his tongue, so that he speaks by Me and his hand so that he takes by Me."

Those who receive guidance from the chapter entitled "Social Affairs" are divided into three parts explained by God in the verse.

> "Then We gave the Scripture as inheritance unto those whom We ele(. of Our bondmen". (35: 32).

(1) Those who acquire the virtue of administering justice on contemplative basis and follow the right middle course between two extremes.

(2) Those who do not appreciate the value of piety and avoid the performance of duty towards their fellow-men belong to the category of the tyrants, and serious afflictions would be dispensed to them.

(3) Those who rise higher and enjoy the rank equivalent to that of the ancient Musiims. In this age of ours it seems impossible that one could belong to this third type, though it is earnestly hoped that the people who can fulfil the conditions laid down for the pious and the just could be raised to this high rank, as explained by the Holy Prophet:

> "The day is not far off, when people who get one tenth of your portion will attain to salvation."

When his companions inquired of him as to how it could be possible, he replied:

> For you help others to do good deeds."

It is wrong to think that the money earned by the farmers or businessmen is always legitimate and that the one who makes use of such money is entitled to the rank enjoyed by the ancient Muslims. It is also incorrect to believe that the persons in the employ of the Government, who receive pay and emoluments are tyrants, for the money earned by the businessmen is inter-mixed, and as such it requires a thorough process of analysis, before it could be properly made use of. Similarly the large fortune at the disposal of the kings also requires a thorough scrutiny and careful investigation. Seen from this point of view a king hoards three kinds of riches:

(1) Money taken from some one by force.

(2) Money collected from the subjects on account of fine or penalty.

(3) Money realise from the subjects on account of tax and revenue at exorbitant rates.

The above-mentioned types of wealth are forbidden. Those kings and *sultans* are, of course, usurpers, and tyrants who accumulate such wealth and do not return it to their real owners. There is a kind of money which is quite legitimate. This is the price of the food-grains grown on one's own farm and disposed of. The goods on money stolen or taken away from others with brute force is illegitimate. This verdict of *Shari'at* is quite clear about this. The one who is in possession of such goods or money should distribute it among the needy, "*dervishes*" or contribute it towards the welfare of the society. It must not be left in the hands of the usurpers who will certainly mis-use it and disturb social justice. If the owners of the money is a *dervish*, he should use as much of it as he is surely in need of. And if he is a rich man, he should not spend a single penny, but should contribute it towards the national reconstruction or the relief of the poor and the needy. If this rich man is really in need of some money, he is allowed to take as much of it as it is required to meet the bare necessities of his family. Mr. So and So has stayed for several years in the Convent adjacent to my home. He bears a good moral character and has discarded his worldly life for the sake of his life Hereafter. If he is too poor to support his family and wants to be benefitted by the *Sultan's* almsgiving or charitable endowments, he ought to secure a religious verdict on this subject in his favour, and avail himself of the concession with the approval of the competent authority. It is very difficult to subject one's self to the religious verdict of a balance (*mizan*) in these hard times and discover whether he and his family really stand in need of financial help from the Government. If there is such a poor man, he deserves to be looked after, instead of being deprived of the monetary assistance which is his due, therefore, it is incumbent on Mr. So and So to seek the help of his Muslim brethren and other *Shaikhs*, who will certainly extend their helping hands, to relieve him out of his financial distress. The peace of Allah be on the Holy Prophet who is the Head and Chief of His Messengers.

Yours sincerely,

Al-Ghazzali.